Zombies, Unicorns, Cannibals

Strange Tales from the Bible

Sébastien Doane

Paulist Press
New York / Mahwah, NJ

© 2018 Novalis Publishing Inc.

Cover design: Martin Gould
Cover image: iStockphoto (Bliznetsov)
Layout: Audrey Wells
Translation: David Doane

Published in the United States by Paulist Press
997 Macarthur Boulevard
Mahwah, NJ 07430
www.paulistpress.com

Originally published by Novalis

Publishing Office
10 Lower Spadina Avenue, Suite 400
Toronto, Ontario, Canada
M5V 2Z2

Head Office
4475 Frontenac Street
Montréal, Québec, Canada
H2H 2S2

www.novalis.ca

Library of Congress Control Number: 2018930363

ISBN 978-0-8091-5405-0 (paperback)

Printed in Canada.

5   4   3   2   1   22   21   20   19   18

Contents

Zombies,
Unicorns,
Cannibals

Introduction
My Passion for the Bible

When I received my first Bible at age twelve, I had no idea it would inspire such a passion in me. At the time, it was compulsory reading for my religion class. I had certainly heard about the Bible in church, but my appetite for biblical stories began when I decided to open the "Good Book." Like many teenagers, sex and violence intrigued me. How could I know that by diving into the scriptures, I was going to find a perfect fit? The first book I devoured was the Song of Songs. Finding sensual poetry in the Bible was a pleasant surprise. To satisfy my curiosity, I turned my attention to the Apocalypse, in the book of Revelation. This was far more difficult to understand. When I got to the end, I was bewildered, but still enjoyed the experience of reading the Bible on my own. After delving into these two biblical books, I was hooked.

Since that time, I have worked my way through every page of the book of books. Unusual stories still particularly interest me – those that are excluded from liturgical celebrations because they are too violent, too vulgar, too sexual, too bizarre, or too far-fetched. And yet these strange tales are part of the Bible, judged as being inspired by God and worthy to be read by believers. When I started ministry work in a high school, I discovered that these stories were an excellent gateway for teens. Most of my students were not the least bit interested in religious matters, but during their free time at noon they would knock on my door and say, "Tell us another story from the Bible! This time, we want an extra bloody one!" Without knowing it, they were at risk of catching my passion for the Bible.

Since publishing my first book (in French) of unusual biblical stories,[1] I realized that this type of narrative also interests adults, whether they are religious or not. That book led to two series of radio programs, articles on www.interbible.org, a university course, and several lectures and workshops. People connect me with strange tales from the Bible to the point that even when I am in a meeting with university professors, if there is some free time, I am asked to tell a biblical story that might surprise them. So I gathered a number of strange tales from the Bible, and now I have the pleasure of sharing some of them with you.

When a Literal Interpretation Leads to Genital Self-mutilation

The various ways of interpreting the Bible occupy an important place in this book. The following is a brief example that demonstrates why it is worth reflecting on how we interpret the Bible.

---

1   *Mais d'où vient la femme de Caïn? Les récits insolites de la Bible*, Montréal/Paris, Novalis/Bayard, 2010.

Do you know Origen? He was a specialist in biblical interpretation who lived at the beginning of the third century. As a young man, he was rigid in interpreting two passages literally: "There are eunuchs who have made themselves eunuchs for the kingdom of heaven" (Matthew 19:12) and "If your hand is for you an occasion of sin, cut it off" (Mark 9:43). Origen castrated himself to escape further temptations. He clearly had a great desire to live in unity with the Scriptures, which is commendable. But this example shows how a literal interpretation of the Bible can be very painful indeed!

Later in life, Origen realized that he should have thought it through before deciding to commit such an act. In his teaching given at Caesarea, he admitted that he regretted his gesture, attributing the error to a literal reading of the Scriptures. He is considered to be the father of biblical exegesis, partly because he developed the theory of the three senses of writing: the literal (carnal, historical) sense, the moral sense (which edifies the soul) and the spiritual sense (mystical or allegorical).[2] For him, every verse in the Bible can be interpreted in various ways. He therefore acknowledged that he could have (and indeed should have) interpreted differently the verses that led to his castration.

Taking certain passages of the Bible literally can lead to other extreme acts, such as killing those who are considered sinners, supposedly for their own good. A literal reading of the Bible is only one interpretation among others. It is easy for atheists, such

---

2   In pursuing the work of Origen, theologians like Jerome, Augustine, and Thomas Aquinas came to speak of four meanings of Scripture. Each theologian has his own way of grouping the different types of interpretation, but all agree that there is more than one meaning to be discovered.

as Richard Dawkins (*The God Delusion*, 2006) or Christopher Hitchens (*God Is Not Great*, 2007), to ridicule the Bible by considering only a literal reading of excerpts taken out of context. Yet not all readers of the Bible are devoid of critical sense. For most Christians, it is not a book of recipes to follow literally, but a work that requires personal and communal reflection.

Instead of trying to get around the difficulty represented by the bizarre, sometimes cruel, sometimes incoherent episodes of the Bible, this book aims to highlight them and to help readers develop an appetite for reading the Bible. The various stories tackled here will hopefully be an initiation to the Bible that is both instructive and playful.

A Question of Method

For each text presented, I have done research that draws on various methods of interpreting the Bible, both historical and literary. But the central method of my approach is called reader response. The aim of this method is to see the text no longer as an object, but as an experience. Reading is a creative activity. The literary work comes to life when the text meets the reader. Traditionally, "the" meaning of a text was whatever interpretation one could make once the book was closed and the reading completed. Yet this "final" interpretation is but one of many. In reading, we constantly make and break expectations, syntheses and reading assumptions that are as important as the interpretations made at the end of the reading experience.

When we emphasize the role of the reader in the interpretative process, it becomes obvious that all the texts are multifaceted. Each word can be interpreted differently by different readers. Similarly, the links between these words give rise to different interpretations. Furthermore, narratives can never tell everything; there are always indeterminate spaces, or gaps, in the text. Readers must therefore make choices and fill in the blanks.

Reader response proposes not to focus on the text itself, but on the interaction that takes place between reader and text. Rather than asking what this passage of the Bible means, this process seeks to discover what the reader experiences when he or she reads a text. Instead of asking what a text means, we can ask, "What does this text do?" One tries to describe what happens when the reader approaches the text actively and constructs its meaning through reading, through its hypotheses and interpretive options.

This method seems to me to be especially appropriate for pastoral work in the Church, since it emphasizes the encounter between the text and the reader – that is, the moment when an ancient text becomes the word of God for today. It can also interest critical readers of the Bible who wish to develop a personal interpretation without necessarily taking courses on Scripture from an academic institution.

Why Read Strange Tales?

Why read these strange tales? First, they are truly captivating. But more importantly, they are the best examples that move us away from a literal, historical or fundamentalist interpretation of the Bible. When a text does not make sense at face value, we cannot take it literally. In a way, the effect of an apparently absurd text projects readers into a quest for meaning, freeing them from fundamentalist reflexes.

For each unusual narrative, after a short presentation, you will have access to the biblical text (New Revised Standard Version). I will then highlight the elements of the text that usually surprise people. To help you try to understand these better, I will place the text in its historical and literary context. Finally, I will offer personal reflections on contemporary issues relating to those dealt with in the biblical stories.

I hope you will have as much pleasure reading these stories as I did.

The Old Testament

A Biblical "Ménage à Trois"

When comparing our culture with that of the Bible, it becomes obvious that the understanding of the act of conception has changed dramatically over time. The biblical version is certainly more visual and has a simpler way of talking about it. As far as the Bible is concerned, it takes at least three to make a baby!

To Each His Own

In biblical culture, the male had everything he needed to produce a child within his seed (*sperma*, in Greek). Women were a mere receptacle, albeit necessary for the proper development of the child. For conception, a third actor was indispensable. It was commonly accepted that the will of God was essential for conception to result from sexual relations. Thus, God always had an important role to play in the birth of a human being.

The First "Ménage à Trois"

[1]Now the man knew his wife Eve, and she conceived and bore Cain, saying, "I have produced a man with

the help of the Lord." [2]Next she bore his brother Abel. Now Abel was a keeper of sheep, and Cain a tiller of the ground. (Genesis 4:1-2)

The Old Testament gives us stories that emphasize the importance of God's role in the conception of children. To accomplish this, the narrative diminishes the role of the male. Since his participation in the conception of a child goes without saying, some texts ignore it completely, accentuating God's role. Let us consider the reaction of Eve, the first woman, after the birth of her first child, Cain: "I have produced a man with the help of the Lord" (Genesis 4:1). It is obvious that the conception of Cain was the result of a sexual relationship between Adam and Eve. "Now the man [Adam] knew his wife Eve, and she conceived and bore Cain" (Genesis 4:1). "Knowing" is an expression commonly used in the Bible to refer to sexual relations. Adam and Eve had a sexual relationship, but it was the grace of God that gave them a child.

Other Biblical Examples

The same applies to Ruth (Ruth 4:13), Leah (Genesis 29:13-32) and Rachel (Genesis 30:22-23); like Eve, these three women became pregnant thanks to God, without explicit mention of any man in the equation.

Isaiah 66:9 says that it is God who opens the way to life. Literally, the Lord opens the womb to deliver a child. It is God who has the power to allow a woman to bear a child or not. In the Bible, therefore, every pregnancy requires a relationship between a man and a woman, but this doesn't happen without the mediation of God.

Conception without Planning

Today, given scientific progress, women are able to conceive children under new conditions. This is great news for infertile couples. But scientific progress has opened a door to all sorts of new developments without first having any real ethical reflection on the subject. Single women and heterosexual and homosexual couples decide on the father of their future child, browsing catalogues of potential parents. A male who has donated sperm may find himself father to scores of children. Women are willing to carry children for others and, since 2015, it is even possible to have children with the genes of three people. All these cases raise ethical questions that need to be discussed.

In general, we want to totally control the conception of children, even within couples who conceive them in the traditional way. The average age of parenting is steadily increasing as the priorities of young adults go first to education, work, money, pleasure, and so on. Family responsibilities and the arrival of children are put on hold.

I do not want to preach on the sensitive subjects of contraception and abortion, but could it be possible to find a little more room for spontaneity, love and God? We want everything to be absolutely perfect for a child coming into our world. But often, surprises are the greatest gifts in life! We all know someone whose presence among us was unexpected, the result of an "accident." We also know that life would not be the same without that little miracle.

Jacob, the First Geneticist

The book of Genesis recounts the misadventures of Jacob while he courted Rachel, the love of his life. He had to work for seven years for Laban, Rachel's father, to win her hand in marriage. Laban deceived Jacob during the wedding ceremony by replacing Rachel with her elder sister, Lea, and so Jacob found himself married to Lea. Since polygamy was a common practice in biblical times, Jacob decided to also marry Rachel, after seven more years of labour for Laban. (This unusual preamble can be found in chapter 29 of Genesis.) However, I chose to examine the next, somewhat lesser known part of this narrative. Here we find Laban still trying to fool Jacob, who manages to turn things to his advantage by using genetic practices that are simply absurd.

> [36]and he set a distance of three days' journey between himself and Jacob, while Jacob was pasturing the rest of Laban's flock.
>
> [37]Then Jacob took fresh rods of poplar and almond and plane, and peeled white streaks in them, exposing the white of the rods. [38]He set the rods that he had peeled in front of the flocks in the troughs, that is, the watering places, where the flocks came to drink. And since they bred when they came to drink, [39]the flocks bred in front of the rods, and so the flocks produced young that were striped, speckled, and spotted. (Genesis 30:36-39)

To stack the deck in his favour, Jacob mates the animals with striped rods in their field of vision. By doing so, the young are born striped, speckled or spotted so that Jacob can take them with him when he leaves.

Of course, genetics – and common sense – tell us that these techniques are impossible. No matter how hard you try, presenting animals with striped images during mating will never affect the genetic makeup that determines the coat of their offspring.

Is It a Miracle?

Faced with this text, it seems we have two options. On the one hand, we can accept this outcome as a miracle. In this way, God renders justice to Jacob, who had been tricked by his father-in-law. On the other hand, we can suppose that our biblical ancestors really believed in these dubious techniques. It seems to me that we have no option but to accept the second alternative, since nothing else in the text orients us toward divine intervention. Furthermore, this narrative clearly shows Jacob's tenacity. He finds a way to succeed by using his own initiatives, despite the obstacles placed in his path. Jacob is a perfect example of someone who can turn the tables in his favour through ingenuity and hard work.

Defeating the System

This narrative presents two characters who try various schemes to defraud each other to get what they consider their due. In life, we have many opportunities to scheme against our fellow citizens or to defraud the system. A good illustration of this can be found in all the investment schemes and banking scandals that led to the recession of 2008. We often hear about people who try to defraud the welfare system or insurance companies, or take advantage of unjustified sick leave. During the 2016 American presidential election, it was announced that one of the candidates defrauded his insurance company by making false claims concerning storm damages to his Florida golf club. The most disturbing thing about this is that a majority of Americans didn't seem to mind, since that candidate won the election.

The problem is that by defrauding the system, we defraud ourselves. It may sound weird, but I am proud to pay my taxes: it is a way to give ourselves collective resources. But we have to have confidence in the integrity of the government and believe that it is using the money wisely. Even in democratic countries, corruption finds its way into the system. History has an unfortunate tendency to repeat itself: like Laban and Jacob, we too often try to pull the wool over the eyes of our fellow citizens.

A Cougar Has Her Eye on Joseph

In our modern culture, a woman who seduces younger men is called a cougar. This is nothing new. Believe it or not, there is a cougar in the book of Genesis, chapter 39. She is married to Potiphar, an Egyptian eunuch who gets failing marks in bed. Potiphar has a servant, Joseph, who could perhaps fulfill his master's marital duties...

> [6]Now Joseph was handsome and good-looking. [7]And after a time his master's wife cast her eyes on Joseph and said, "Lie with me." [8]But he refused and said to his master's wife, "Look, with me here, my master has no concern about anything in the house, and he has put everything that he has in my hand. [9]He is not greater in this house than I am, nor has he kept back anything from me except yourself, because you are his wife. How then could I do this great wickedness, and sin against God?" [10]And although she spoke to Joseph day after day, he would not consent to lie beside her or to be with her. [11]One day, however, when he went into the house to do his work, and while no one else was in the house, [12]she caught hold of his garment, saying, "Lie with me!" But he left his garment in her hand, and fled and ran outside. [13]When she saw that he had left his garment in

her hand and had fled outside, [14]she called out to the members of her household and said to them, "See, my husband has brought among us a Hebrew to insult us! He came in to me to lie with me, and I cried out with a loud voice; [15]and when he heard me raise my voice and cry out, he left his garment beside me, and fled outside." [16]Then she kept his garment by her until his master came home, [17]and she told him the same story, saying, "The Hebrew servant, whom you have brought among us, came in to me to insult me; [18]but as soon as I raised my voice and cried out, he left his garment beside me, and fled outside."

[19]When his master heard the words that his wife spoke to him, saying, "This is the way your servant treated me," he became enraged. [20]And Joseph's master took him and put him into the prison, the place where the king's prisoners were confined; he remained there in prison. (Genesis 39:6-20)

The Muslim and Jewish traditions have given the name of Zuleika to this anonymous woman of questionable morals. While some men complain that women are complicated and hard to comprehend, this does not apply to the wife of Potiphar. The woman in this narrative knows exactly what she wants and expresses it concisely, saying to Joseph twice, "Lie with me." She even takes off his clothing.

The Consequences of Zuleika's Passion

This is a classic case of adultery. Polygamy was permitted in biblical times, but polyandry wasn't. A married woman could not have sex with man who was not her husband. In this case, the woman is married to a eunuch. In the Bible, the word "eunuch" can have multiple meanings. He may be a man who is castrated, effeminate, transgender, impotent or incapable of fathering a child. In general, eunuchs were in the service of a king or queen to keep guard over their harem. Perhaps Potiphar's wife did not want Joseph solely for sexual pleasure. It is entirely possible that she wanted to have children, something very important at the time, and something her husband could not give her.

According to Jewish legend, Joseph's beauty was the motivation behind Zuleika's behaviour. The legend recounts that the women of Egypt mocked Zuleika's desire to "lie with" a Hebrew slave. One day when she invited them to her house, all the women were cutting apples. When Joseph entered the room, they were so distracted by his beauty, the women accidentally cut each other's fingers. We can think what we want about this legend, but an excellent argument in favour of that interpretation is found in the Bible. The biblical passage in question begins with a clear affirmation of Joseph's beauty.

From Cougar to Mystic

Most commentators present Zuleika as a sinner, a wicked woman. Indeed, according to the Bible, it is she who causes Joseph to be arrested under false pretenses. Dante's *Divine Comedy* places Potiphar's wife in the eighth circle of hell, with those who have committed fraud and adultery.

Other voices offer a much more lenient interpretation. According to the Sufi mystic poet Rumi, Zuleika's carnal obsession is a manifestation of her deep desire for God. For Rumi, the desire for God is present whenever a person loves another. This interpretation is a good example of what is known as a spiritual interpretation of a text. It distances itself from the primary meaning of the biblical text to convey a way to enter into a relationship with God.

Destroyed and Saved by a Garment

In the previous chapter of Genesis, chapter 37, Joseph had experienced a series of setbacks because of a garment he had received from his father. That misadventure led to his slavery in Egypt. In chapter 39, the wife of Potiphar takes his garment and uses it to accuse and imprison him. In prison, Joseph interprets the dreams of the officers in charge and eventually is asked to do the same for the Pharaoh. Because of his success in this endeavour, Joseph is given great power in Egypt. He is thus able to welcome his family when they seek refuge there during a famine. The biblical narratives concerning Joseph have an obvious purpose: to get from Canaan to Egypt, from the book of Genesis to the book of Exodus, from the Patriarchs to Moses. In the end, the accusation of Potiphar's wife allowed for what was perceived as God's plan for his chosen people to be realized.

Where to Draw the Line?

The accusations of Potiphar's wife are still commonplace today. False sexual assault charges are a good way to ruin someone's life. Rape is such a horrible act that once a person is charged with this crime, the accused loses their reputation. For a teacher, a priest, a police officer or a doctor, for example, false accusations can ruin a career. Every precaution must be taken to discover the truth. As a consequence, society often overreacts. For example, in training courses for school bus drivers, instructors warn future drivers not to touch the students under any circumstances. Even if a kindergarten child falls while climbing onto a bus, the driver should not offer a helping hand. It is difficult to know where to draw the line, but, in this case, it seems society has taken caution beyond reasonable limits.

Protected by the Blood of the Foreskin

The story where Moses encounters the Lord at the burning bush (Exodus 3) contains some unusual elements. The Lord sets out to prove his power through amazing feats. First, God transforms a stick into a snake (4:1-5). Then he causes leprosy to develop on Moses' hand (4:6-7). Finally, as astonishing as it may seem, the Lord hardens the heart of Pharaoh so that God's chosen people cannot leave Egypt (4:21). I want to draw attention to what happens when Moses and his family set off on their trek back to Egypt.

> 24On the way, at a place where they spent the night, the Lord met him and tried to kill him. 25But Zipporah took a flint and cut off her son's foreskin, and touched Moses's feet with it, and said, "Truly you are a bridegroom of blood to me!" 26So he let him alone. It was then she said, "A bridegroom of blood by circumcision." (Exodus 4:24-26)

What?! Without further explanation, we are told that the Lord wanted to kill Moses? Why? Just a few verses before, he had convinced Moses to go back to Egypt to free God's people from slavery! Moses accepted the challenge and, at the first opportunity, the Lord tries to put him to death? How can this be?

The Lord of Combat

Could the narrator be making a connection between this narrative and the story from the book of Genesis (32:25-33) where Jacob encounters God and battles with him? Christians have often understood that enigmatic story as an allegory of their spiritual warfare in the face of the mystery of God. From the Jewish perspective, it is a narrative supporting the etymology of the word "Israel," which means "fighting with God." When we consider these narratives side by side, they give the impression that an encounter with the Lord can be a dangerous affair.

Saved by the Blood of the Foreskin

Zipporah, the non-Jewish wife of Moses, protects her husband with blood from the foreskin of their child. Anyone acquainted with the book of Exodus can't help but see a link with the blood of the paschal lamb used to mark the doors of the Hebrews – blood that protected them when the Lord decided to kill the children of the Egyptians (Exodus 12). Rabbis from the second century AD used this account to show the importance of observing the rite of circumcision. Rashi, an expert on biblical texts living in the eleventh century, proposed that Moses deserved death because he failed to circumcise his son.

To make things even more bizarre, I must mention that the word "foot" in the Bible is often a euphemism for the male sex organ. Thus, taking into consideration this meaning of "foot," Moses is protected because his wife brushes his penis with the blood of their son's foreskin. Although interesting, this interpretation does nothing to help us understand the narrative.

The God of Death?

Even today, people see God as the cause of suffering and death. For example, when someone dies, they often say that God took the person before his or her time. Is it really God who decides the hour of our death? Some say yes, since God knows everything. Yet this position has the disadvantage of leading to a determinism that restricts human freedom. Moreover, even if God knows the way we are going to die, it does not make him the cause of our death. The God of the Bible is above all the God of life.

Do Rituals Save?

Rituals and superstitions are still used to protect us from misfortune. Many tales could seem to justify such practices. Yet these superstitious rituals contain little substance when we open ourselves to biblical texts about salvation. For example, in the Gospel of Matthew (chapter 25), the criterion of divine judgment is found in the attitude of the believer toward the "little ones" in society. As far as Paul is concerned, it is faith that saves believers. Rituals can fulfill many functions and can be a great way to profess our faith, but should they be motivated by a fear of God?

If you ever feel that the Lord is out to get you, cutting the foreskin of your child for protection might not be such a great idea. It would be far better to seriously review the way you perceive God!

How to Test Your Wife's Fidelity

Are you a jealous husband? If so, here is an inspirational text just for you. On the other hand, if you are a woman, you will probably find this revolting. How does the Bible propose to test a woman's fidelity? Keep reading!

[11]The Lord spoke to Moses, saying: [12]Speak to the Israelites and say to them: If any man's wife goes astray and is unfaithful to him, [13]if a man has had intercourse with her but it is hidden from her husband, so that she is undetected though she has defiled herself, and there is no witness against her since she was not caught in the act; [14]if a spirit of jealousy comes on him, and he is jealous of his wife who has defiled herself; or if a spirit of jealousy comes on him, and he is jealous of his wife, though she has not defiled herself; [15]then the man shall bring his wife to the priest. And he shall bring the offering required for her, one-tenth of an ephah of barley flour. He shall pour no oil on it and put no frankincense on it, for it is a grain offering of jealousy, a grain offering of remembrance, bringing iniquity to remembrance.

[16]Then the priest shall bring her near, and set her before the Lord; [17]the priest shall take holy water in an earthen vessel, and take some of the dust that is on the

floor of the tabernacle and put it into the water. [18]The priest shall set the woman before the Lord, dishevel the woman's hair, and place in her hands the grain offering of remembrance, which is the grain offering of jealousy. In his own hand the priest shall have the water of bitterness that brings the curse. [19]Then the priest shall make her take an oath, saying, "If no man has lain with you, if you have not turned aside to uncleanness while under your husband's authority, be immune to this water of bitterness that brings the curse. [20]But if you have gone astray while under your husband's authority, if you have defiled yourself and some man other than your husband has had intercourse with you," [21]—let the priest make the woman take the oath of the curse and say to the woman—"the Lord make you an execration and an oath among your people, when the Lord makes your uterus drop, your womb discharge; [22]now may this water that brings the curse enter your bowels and make your womb discharge, your uterus drop!" And the woman shall say, "Amen. Amen."

[23]Then the priest shall put these curses in writing, and wash them off into the water of bitterness. [24]He shall make the woman drink the water of bitterness that brings the curse, and the water that brings the curse shall enter her and cause bitter pain. [25]The priest shall take the grain offering of jealousy out of the woman's hand, and shall elevate the grain offering before the Lord and bring it to the altar; [26]and the priest shall take

a handful of the grain offering, as its memorial portion, and turn it into smoke on the altar, and afterward shall make the woman drink the water. [27]When he has made her drink the water, then, if she has defiled herself and has been unfaithful to her husband, the water that brings the curse shall enter into her and cause bitter pain, and her womb shall discharge, her uterus drop, and the woman shall become an execration among her people. [28]But if the woman has not defiled herself and is clean, then she shall be immune and be able to conceive children.

[29]This is the law in cases of jealousy, when a wife, while under her husband's authority, goes astray and defiles herself, [30]or when a spirit of jealousy comes on a man and he is jealous of his wife; then he shall set the woman before the Lord, and the priest shall apply this entire law to her. [31]The man shall be free from iniquity, but the woman shall bear her iniquity. (Numbers 5:11-31)

This test of marital fidelity is the word of the Lord? It shows that the Bible contains texts written by men and for men. And, in this case, for married men who suspect their wife of infidelity.

The recipe is simple: if you doubt your wife's fidelity, bring her to the priest so he can give her a bitter drink, a toxic liquid. The expression used in the book of Exodus (15:23) designates water that people in the desert refuse to drink because it is unfit for consumption.

This rite is not exclusive to the Bible. The judgments of God called "ordeal" were ancient eastern practices, also found in

Europe during the Middle Ages. When there was no evidence to accuse someone, a comparable rite could lead to a conviction or an acquittal. This practice most certainly had its origins in the domain of magic, and was reinterpreted by the Bible to create a religious practice approved by the Lord.

What About the Woman?

From a woman's point of view, this text is disturbing. The only time a woman is allowed to speak is not to defend herself or to explain herself, but to say, "Amen, Amen," to accept the words spoken against her by the priest. And by doing so, she apparently accepts that her belly will swell and her intestines will wither and die. I doubt this is really what the woman in question would want…

The last verse is particularly shocking: "The man shall be free from iniquity." Even if the test reveals that the woman was falsely accused, she is not allowed to say or do anything against her husband, who has total immunity. To make things worse, there is no punishment for unfaithful men. This is not surprising. In the culture of the Bible, polygamy was accepted, and a man could sleep with any woman, provided she was not married to another man.

And Then?

The above narrative simply adds that a guilty woman will have to accept the consequences of her failings. The problem is that death is the sentence associated with adultery, and it must be administered to the woman in question (Leviticus 20:10,

Deuteronomy 22:22-24, Ezekiel 16:38-40). Normally, execution is by stoning (Deuteronomy 22:20-22).

Honour Crimes

Of course, this kind of test is no longer practised today. But men continue to judge and even kill women who behave in ways that they deem deviant. For example, in Canada, the sisters Zainab, Sahar and Geeti Shafia, as well as Rona Amir Mohamed, were murdered by family members because they "dishonoured" their family in the ways they dressed and talked to men. These women lived a few blocks from my home. They were found at the bottom of the Rideau Canal in Kingston. It is easy to say that this example comes from a Muslim family that failed to integrate into Canadian society. Yet other events show that societies must solve the problem of violence against women. In Quebec, fourteen women were murdered during the Polytechnique massacre in 1989. Since that event, 1,500 Quebecers have been murdered by their former spouses. It is easy to close our eyes, insisting that the violence in the book of Numbers belongs to another culture. In reality, spousal abuse is out of control. A step in the right direction would be to denounce all forms of violence against women. Zero tolerance!

A Talkative Donkey Experiences God

Animals speak their mind in several stories in the Bible. The first that comes to mind is the serpent from the book of Genesis, who is the force behind Eve tasting the forbidden fruit (Genesis 3). In the following account there is a talkative donkey, but unlike the serpent, this animal plays a sympathetic role.

[21]So Balaam got up in the morning, saddled his donkey, and went with the officials of Moab.

[22]God's anger was kindled because he was going, and the angel of the Lord took his stand in the road as his adversary. Now he was riding on the donkey, and his two servants were with him. [23]The donkey saw the angel of the Lord standing in the road, with a drawn sword in his hand; so the donkey turned off the road, and went into the field; and Balaam struck the donkey, to turn it back onto the road. [24]Then the angel of the Lord stood in a narrow path between the vineyards, with a wall on either side. [25]When the donkey saw the angel of the Lord, it scraped against the wall, and scraped Balaam's foot against the wall; so he struck it again. [26]Then the angel of the Lord went ahead, and stood in a narrow place, where there was no way to turn either to the right or to the left. [27]When the donkey saw the angel

of the Lord, it lay down under Balaam; and Balaam's anger was kindled, and he struck the donkey with his staff. [28]Then the Lord opened the mouth of the donkey, and it said to Balaam, "What have I done to you, that you have struck me these three times?" [29]Balaam said to the donkey, "Because you have made a fool of me! I wish I had a sword in my hand! I would kill you right now!" [30]But the donkey said to Balaam, "Am I not your donkey, which you have ridden all your life to this day? Have I been in the habit of treating you this way?" And he said, "No."

[31]Then the Lord opened the eyes of Balaam, and he saw the angel of the Lord standing in the road, with his drawn sword in his hand; and he bowed down, falling on his face. [32]The angel of the Lord said to him, "Why have you struck your donkey these three times? I have come out as an adversary, because your way is perverse before me. [33]The donkey saw me, and turned away from me these three times. If it had not turned away from me, surely just now I would have killed you and let it live." [34]Then Balaam said to the angel of the Lord, "I have sinned, for I did not know that you were standing in the road to oppose me. Now therefore, if it is displeasing to you, I will return home." (Numbers 22:21-34)

Who Is This Angel of the Lord?

The Old Testament commonly uses this expression to designate God without naming him directly. It is a writing technique that allows God to react to a situation, while safeguarding his spiritual state.

Urban Legends

Why is Balaam in danger of death if he touches the Angel of the Lord? This is one of many "urban legends" about God that have become part of the biblical culture. Several texts in the Bible indicate that seeing God can lead to death. In this account, this is precisely the reason why Balaam cannot see God. If he could, he would already be dead! Even touching God can lead to the same fatal result. Another biblical account (2 Samuel 6:3-10) tells of the death of someone who touched the Ark of the Covenant in an effort to prevent it from falling to the ground. God is so great, so beyond our human state, that the mere fact of seeing or touching God results in death.

The Donkey, a Spiritual Guide

Curiously, this restriction must not apply to donkeys, since the animal clearly sees the manifestation of God. The donkey allows itself to be beaten by its master to prevent contact with the Angel of the Lord. In our culture, donkeys are often perceived as stupid, with a stubborn streak. But in the world of the Bible, they are presented positively. The donkey is a beast used for work and, above all, a travelling companion par excellence. Jesus enters Jerusalem on a donkey, echoing the prophet Zechariah (9:9), who evoked the humility of a peaceful messiah mounted on a donkey. In Balaam's account, the donkey sees the Angel of the Lord, while the prophet does not. In short, it appears that donkeys are more capable of discerning God's presence than humans are. Even though the presence of a donkey and a cow in the crib is not biblical, some interpretations link Balaam's donkey to the donkey in the stable, implying that it could better perceive the true identity of Jesus than the humans in the story could.

Seeing God

The passage about Balaam's donkey helps us to identify the literary genre used in this excerpt from the book of Numbers. Normally, in historical narratives, we do not find animals capable of speaking. What we are dealing with here is obviously a text akin to a fable. Its purpose is to convey a message, and is not intended to be taken literally. And what is this message? Without a doubt it is an encouragement to look for the presence of God in the world around us and to give that presence the respect it deserves.

Witnessing to the presence of God is not a commonplace event; it is difficult to perceive in our lives. Like Balaam, I do not see God with my eyes. Furthermore, I tend to be wary of those who see God everywhere, as if God's presence was self-evident. Discernment is a must. I have learned to look back on my life to see how God might have been present without my knowing it, and certainly without my seeing him.

Stopping the Sun to Condemn Galileo

According to the book of Joshua, when the chosen people entered the Promised Land (Canaan) after the long journey across the desert, they were faced with the task of dislodging the inhabitants to take the land the Lord had promised them. During the battles, the Israelites made a pact with the Gibeonites. Faced with a common enemy, the Amorites, Joshua and his army rescued the city of Gibeon. This is the story of that cosmic battle:

> [11]As they fled before Israel, while they were going down the slope of Beth-horon, the Lord threw down huge stones from heaven on them as far as Azekah, and they died; there were more who died because of the hailstones than the Israelites killed with the sword. [12]On the day when the Lord gave the Amorites over to the Israelites, Joshua spoke to the Lord; and he said in the sight of Israel, "Sun, stand still at Gibeon, and Moon, in the valley of Aijalon."
>
> [13]And the sun stood still, and the moon stopped, until the nation took vengeance on their enemies.
>
> Is this not written in the Book of Jashar? The sun stopped in midheaven, and did not hurry to set for about a whole day. [14]There has been no day like it before

or since, when the Lord heeded a human voice; for the Lord fought for Israel. ¹⁵Then Joshua returned, and all Israel with him, to the camp at Gilgal.

¹⁶Meanwhile, these five kings fled and hid themselves in the cave at Makkedah. ¹⁷And it was told Joshua, "The five kings have been found, hidden in the cave at Makkedah." (Joshua 10:11-17)

Several elements of this excerpt are strange: the Lord attacking with a rain of stones, the reference to a mysterious book, and then the stopping of the sun and the moon.

The Sky Is Falling on Our Heads!

The battles in the book of Joshua are theological ones. The main theme is this: God is faithful to the promises he makes to his people. He provides them with a homeland by helping them destroy their enemies. The text is clear. Not only does God endorse this war, but also he takes part in it, siding with Israel. The stones thrown by God, resembling hailstones, are effective indeed. They succeed in killing more Amorites than Joshua's army does. We are far from the image of a God of peace who seeks happiness for all! The role of God in this story is clear. He is the God of a particular nation (Israel), and as any good warrior would do, he fights their enemies. Does this come as a surprise? In the culture of the ancient Near East, it was believed that the gods came to fight with the army of those who invoked them. Thus, warriors brought to the battlefield statues and other religious objects. Something similar is seen in the books of Samuel and the books of Kings, when the Ark of the

Covenant is carried onto the battlefield as a sign of the presence of YHWH, the national God of Israel.

A Mysterious Book

This narrative refers to what some Bible translations call the Book of the Just. What exactly is this mysterious book? We do not know. Other biblical texts also made use of unknown books. For example, 2 Samuel 1:18 refers to what some translations call the "Song of the Bow." Could this be the same book with a different title, caused by a faulty translation of the original Hebrew? In any case, these collections have disappeared. The purpose of using these references is to show that the actions that take place in the narrative are the fulfillment of prophecies.

Stopping the Sun and the Moon

Following Joshua's order, the sun and the moon stopped their trajectory for an entire day. Commenting on this story, the book of Sirach (46:4) writes that "one day [became] as long as two." This extraordinary event seems to have awarded victory to Joshua. The text itself indicates that something unusual occurred. It mentions that there was never a day that compared to this one. But contrary to the surprise of the contemporary reader when faced with the inertia of the sun and the moon, the author clarifies that the astonishing element is rather the fact that a man ordered the Lord to act on his behalf. To justify this small breach of theological rules, the narrator explains that the Lord was fighting for Israel.

Reading the Bible to Understand the Sky

In the seventeenth century, opponents of the Italian intellectual Galileo Galilei used this biblical passage as a theological weapon against him. Galileo's observations on the movements of the stars supported Copernicus' thesis, which encouraged adopting heliocentrism – the thesis that the sun is stable and that the other celestial bodies, including the earth, revolve around it. Galileo's ideas clashed with those of Aristotle's followers, who supported a stable geocentrism. Indeed, until the time of Galileo, common sense saw the earth as immutable, with the rest of the celestial bodies revolving around it. During Galileo's famous trial, two passages of the Bible were evoked as "proofs" that the earth was immutable: this excerpt from the book of Joshua (10:13), which states that "the sun stopped and the moon stopped," and the first verse of Psalm 93:1: "He has established the world; it shall never be moved." Galileo's opponents judged his theses on the basis of their literal interpretation of these verses. For them, the Bible could not err.

At the end of his trial, the Congregation of the Holy Office, the judicial arm of the Inquisition, sentenced Galileo to life imprisonment. He was ordered to reject the heliocentric system of Copernicus, whose work had been banned by the Church fifteen years earlier. Pope Urban VII, who had supported Galileo at the outset, eventually transmuted this sentence to a house arrest.

Reflections

In the eighteenth century, Benedict XV lifted the prohibitions surrounding the works of Galileo. Under John Paul II, the

Church embraced them in 1992. Here are two excerpts from the speech of this pope:

> Thus, today's science, with its methods and the freedom of research it entails, obliged theologians to question their own criteria for the interpretation of Scripture. Most did not do it.

> Paradoxically, Galileo, a sincere believer, was more perspicacious on this point than his opponents. "If Scripture cannot err," he wrote to Benedetto Castelli, "some of its interpreters and commentators can, and did so in many ways."[3]

Nowadays, it is clear how Galileo's methods, based on observation, challenged a literal way of reading the Bible. His condemnation also prompts us to reflect on our ways of interpreting the holy book. Galileo's opponents firmly believed that their interpretation of the Bible was the truth and not a mere interpretation. Instead of trying to convince Galileo by rational arguments, they played the card of authority. By using their political and religious power, his adversaries imposed their interpretation as truth.

This is a good lesson of humility for the institutional Church and its scriptural interpreters. It is not because we are professors, priests, scripture scholars, doctors or bishops that our interpretation of the Bible is the truth. Our interpretation must be validated other than by the authority argument. All we can do is try to persuade others of our way of reading a text.

---

3 Excerpts from Pope John Paul II's speech to the Pontifical Academy of Sciences, October 31, 1992.

Here are three criteria that might be used in judging an interpretation:

1. Return to the text. The most effective way to judge an interpretation is to go back and read the narrative carefully to see if the interpretation has clear support in the text.

2. Seek the opinion of others. Do those around us (family, church, university, etc.) recognize themselves in the interpretation? Collective vigilance helps to identify interpretations that are not well grounded. As the saying goes, "Two heads are better than one."

3. Follow Tradition. Many centuries of reading the Bible have given us a rich history of biblical interpretations. It is always a good approach to situate our own interpretation among those who have gone before us.

A Daughter Sacrificed for Victory

The book of Judges tells of a troubled period in the history of Israel. The twelve tribes are struggling to remain united and are constantly at war with their neighbours. This is the account of what Jephthah, the military leader of the Hebrews, did to triumph over the Ammonites.

[30] And Jephthah made a vow to the Lord, and said, "If you will give the Ammonites into my hand, [31] then whoever comes out of the doors of my house to meet me, when I return victorious from the Ammonites, shall be the Lord's, to be offered up by me as a burnt offering." [32] So Jephthah crossed over to the Ammonites to fight against them; and the Lord gave them into his hand. [33] He inflicted a massive defeat on them from Aroer to the neighborhood of Minnith, twenty towns, and as far as Abel-keramim. So the Ammonites were subdued before the people of Israel.

[34] Then Jephthah came to his home at Mizpah; and there was his daughter coming out to meet him with timbrels and with dancing. She was his only child; he had no son or daughter except her. [35] When he saw her, he tore his clothes, and said, "Alas, my daughter! You have brought me very low; you have become the cause of great trouble

to me. For I have opened my mouth to the Lord, and I cannot take back my vow." ³⁶She said to him, "My father, if you have opened your mouth to the Lord, do to me according to what has gone out of your mouth, now that the Lord has given you vengeance against your enemies, the Ammonites." ³⁷And she said to her father, "Let this thing be done for me: Grant me two months, so that I may go and wander on the mountains, and bewail my virginity, my companions and I." ³⁸"Go," he said and sent her away for two months. So she departed, she and her companions, and bewailed her virginity on the mountains. ³⁹At the end of two months, she returned to her father, who did with her according to the vow he had made. She had never slept with a man. So there arose an Israelite custom that ⁴⁰for four days every year the daughters of Israel would go out to lament the daughter of Jephthah the Gileadite.

There is no question of whether a vow of this kind is legitimate. There appears to be no alternative. What has been said must be accomplished. However, the book of Leviticus (27:1-6) teaches that when a daughter is devoted to God, her father can place ten shekels of silver in the sanctuary to free her from a vow offered to the Lord. Was Jephthah so cheap that he did not want to pay the price? Was this exchange proposed by the book of Leviticus still valid? We do not know, but the narrative offers no other alternative than to sacrifice the girl. The message of the story: pay attention to what you promise God.

From Dancing to Death

The joyful dancing of the girl, on the one hand, and her fate, on the other, present the reader with an overwhelming contrast. When we meet her for the first time, we experience a sense of uneasiness, knowing the fate of the first person Jephthah will encounter.

The girl's virginity is considered her greatest misfortune. Contemporary readers are led to believe that the sadness in the text comes from the fact that she will not know love or the fulfillment of a sexual relationship. Yet, in this context, the curse is rather the dishonour of not marrying and, above all, of having no children.

It is interesting that we feel greater empathy for the girl than for the twenty Ammonite towns destroyed by Jephthah and for the people who lived there. Since the story is presented from Israel's perspective, the death of the sons of Ammon seems much less important than the death of Jephthah's daughter. Even today, the daughters of Israel weep over the death of this young virgin.

Negotiating with God

Have you ever negotiated or bargained with God in prayer? It seems like a natural reflex when we receive bad news or when something difficult happens and we have no control over it. Before major league baseball players bat or pitch, we often see them praying or making the sign of the cross. In Montreal, when the Canadiens get to the NHL playoffs, some fans climb the hundreds of steps of St. Joseph's Oratory on their knees before a game to make sure luck is on their side. This example may be a silly one, but when we are facing death or serious illness, we are often willing to try anything: "If you cure me, Lord, I am ready to do the impossible for you." But is it God who causes disease? Is it God who cures the sick? Ultimately, we all will die; bargaining with God cannot change that. God did not intervene to save Jesus from suffering and dying on the cross. Fortunately, as a Christian, my hope is that, like he did with Jesus, God will resurrect me after I die. Death and suffering are part of life, but God is stronger than death.

Personally, I am horrified by the attitude of Jephthah. When a religion or an ideology leads to death, we must be outraged and adjust our way of thinking. Jewish and Christian traditions contain violent narratives like this one, but as readers we are invited simply to say no. The narrator does not take a position, but Jephthah admits that he has said too much. Yes, that is true, but his actions were beyond reason as well! Sacrifices are at the heart of the covenant between God and humankind in the Old Testament. Stories such as the intended sacrifice of Isaac by Abraham (Genesis 22:1-19) show how human sacrifices were replaced by animal sacrifices. The New Covenant introduces a completely different relationship between God and humanity. Jesus died on the cross – Christians interpret this gesture as the ultimate sacrifice.

Gang Banging and Dismemberment

This is one of the most difficult biblical stories to read, because it vividly describes the horrific sexual assault of an innocent person.

[1]In those days, when there was no king in Israel, a certain Levite, residing in the remote parts of the hill country of Ephraim, took to himself a concubine from Bethlehem in Judah. [2]But his concubine became angry with him, and she went away from him to her father's house at Bethlehem in Judah, and was there some four months. [3]Then her husband set out after her, to speak tenderly to her and bring her back. He had with him his servant and a couple of donkeys. When he reached her father's house, the girl's father saw him and came with joy to meet him. [4]His father-in-law, the girl's father, made him stay, and he remained with him three days; so they ate and drank, and he stayed there. [5]On the fourth day they got up early in the morning, and he prepared to go; but the girl's father said to his son-in-law, "Fortify yourself with a bit of food, and after that you may go." [6]So the two men sat and ate and drank together; and the girl's father said to the man, "Why not spend the night and enjoy yourself?" [7]When the man got up to

go, his father-in-law kept urging him until he spent the night there again. [8]On the fifth day he got up early in the morning to leave; and the girl's father said, "Fortify yourself." So they lingered until the day declined, and the two of them ate and drank. [9]When the man with his concubine and his servant got up to leave, his father-in-law, the girl's father, said to him, "Look, the day has worn on until it is almost evening. Spend the night. See, the day has drawn to a close. Spend the night here and enjoy yourself. Tomorrow you can get up early in the morning for your journey, and go home."

[10]But the man would not spend the night; he got up and departed, and arrived opposite Jebus (that is, Jerusalem). He had with him a couple of saddled donkeys, and his concubine was with him. [11]When they were near Jebus, the day was far spent, and the servant said to his master, "Come now, let us turn aside to this city of the Jebusites, and spend the night in it." [12]But his master said to him, "We will not turn aside into a city of foreigners, who do not belong to the people of Israel; but we will continue on to Gibeah." [13]Then he said to his servant, "Come, let us try to reach one of these places, and spend the night at Gibeah or at Ramah." [14]So they passed on and went their way; and the sun went down on them near Gibeah, which belongs to Benjamin. [15]They turned aside there, to go in and spend the night at Gibeah. He went in and sat down in the open square of the city, but no one took them in to spend the night.

[16]Then at evening there was an old man coming from his work in the field. The man was from the hill country of Ephraim, and he was residing in Gibeah. (The people of the place were Benjaminites.) [17]When the old man looked up and saw the wayfarer in the open square of the city, he said, "Where are you going and where do you come from?" [18]He answered him, "We are passing from Bethlehem in Judah to the remote parts of the hill country of Ephraim, from which I come. I went to Bethlehem in Judah; and I am going to my home. Nobody has offered to take me in. [19]We your servants have straw and fodder for our donkeys, with bread and wine for me and the woman and the young man along with us. We need nothing more." [20]The old man said, "Peace be to you. I will care for all your wants; only do not spend the night in the square." [21]So he brought him into his house, and fed the donkeys; they washed their feet, and ate and drank.

[22]While they were enjoying themselves, the men of the city, a perverse lot, surrounded the house, and started pounding on the door. They said to the old man, the master of the house, "Bring out the man who came into your house, so that we may have intercourse with him." [23]And the man, the master of the house, went out to them and said to them, "No, my brothers, do not act so wickedly. Since this man is my guest, do not do this vile thing. [24]Here are my virgin daughter and his concubine; let me bring them out now. Ravish them and do whatever you want to them; but against this man do not

do such a vile thing." [25]But the men would not listen to him. So the man seized his concubine, and put her out to them. They wantonly raped her, and abused her all through the night until the morning. And as the dawn began to break, they let her go. [26]As morning appeared, the woman came and fell down at the door of the man's house where her master was, until it was light.

[27]In the morning her master got up, opened the doors of the house, and when he went out to go on his way, there was his concubine lying at the door of the house, with her hands on the threshold. [28]"Get up," he said to her, "we are going." But there was no answer. Then he put her on the donkey; and the man set out for his home. [29]When he had entered his house, he took a knife, and grasping his concubine he cut her into twelve pieces, limb by limb, and sent her throughout all the territory of Israel. [30]Then he commanded the men whom he sent, saying, "Thus shall you say to all the Israelites, 'Has such a thing ever happened since the day that the Israelites came up from the land of Egypt until this day? Consider it, take counsel, and speak out.'" (Judges 19)

The Absence of a King, a Source of Violence

One way to understand the violence in this story is to see the first verse as the key to the entire chapter: "In those days, when there was no king in Israel…" (Judges 19:1). In this phrase, the narrator explains that the absence of a king has left society vulnerable to unspeakable violence. This refrain is also repeated at the end of the book of Judges (21:25): "In those days there was no king in Israel: all the people did what was right in their own eyes." The vacancy on the throne created problems of morality; each citizen took justice into their own hands. As such, the narrative can be understood as an argument for dismantling the tribal structure in favour of the monarchy. Violence is a means to an end, and therefore justified. To fulfill this function, the text must be as violent as possible to show that the people are in great need of a king, a leader. Of course, this explanation will not satisfy a reader who empathizes with the woman who is raped and murdered.

A reader could have a completely opposite view, challenging the narrator's ideological perspective. This reader could respond to the previous interpretation by noting that even when Israel was ruled by a king, things were not much better. For example, one can think of the rape of Tamar, the sister of Absalom, which takes place in the palace of David (2 Samuel 13) or the adultery and murder committed by David himself, to have Bathsheba (2 Samuel 11). Although some examples of violence are less disturbing than others, life under royalty in Israel, as presented in the books of Kings and the books of Samuel, was no more peaceful than life in the time of the book of Judges.

The Woman's Perspective

I prefer to read this text from the woman's point of view: she is the focal point of a narrative that doesn't give her a name and doesn't even allow her to speak. This woman is more than just a victim. She is a symbol of resistance for any innocent person who is suffering from violence. At the beginning of the narrative, she takes an active role. She gets angry (we do not know why) and leaves her husband. This gesture, which is unusual in such a culture, already shows a determination that will manifest itself once again later in the narrative. When the Levite arrives at her father's house looking for his wife, she lets him in, but does not take part in the dialogue that ensues between her father and her husband.

When it is time to leave, the donkeys are considered before any mention of the woman, suggesting that she is less important than them. The narrative doesn't say whether the woman wanted to stay with her father or to return with her husband. When the men of the city want to sexually assault the Levite, he seizes his concubine and forces her outside. The narration passes very quickly from the security of the interior to the danger on the outside. The reader is not given access to the woman's emotions, but gets the impression that the Levite had no choice but to sacrifice his concubine, whereas in the parallel narrative of Sodom, Lot goes outside to show resistance to the people of the city (Genesis 19:6). The men "raped" the woman, "abused her" and abandoned her (v. 25), intending to break her body and spirit.

One can understand the effort the woman made to return to the entrance of the house (v. 26) as an act of resistance. By doing this, she let her husband and the elderly man know that she was not a victim but a survivor. In her effort to react against the aggression done to her, she places her hands on the threshold of the doorway – a mute appeal addressed to her husband, who remained inside and slept soundly until morning. The sight of this inert body stretched out in a silent cry has virtually no effect on the Levite. The woman has been broken so that the door can remain intact and protect him. Her body represents a border not to be crossed, which protects her husband from rape and death. Ready to continue his journey after the night with the old man, the Levite sees his wife lying at his door. For the first time in the story, he speaks to her: "Get up," he says, "we are going" (v. 28).

This command implies that he believes she is still alive. Yet the woman remains silent, her body broken by aggression. There is a stunning contrast between the Levite's insensitivity and the woman's suffering. The narrator goes on to explain that the Levite puts her on his donkey and takes her home. Once home, he takes his knife and cuts her body into twelve pieces (v. 29). The text is not clear here: did the woman die as a result of the violence done to her in the city, or by her husband's knife? If she was still alive, she would have been expecting his help – so if he murdered her, this was a further desecration of her. He then appealed to the other tribes for a call to war. The gang banging and the dismemberment of the woman are a metaphor for the dismemberment of the people, described in chapters 20 and 21 of the book of Judges. The description of this war explains that tens of thousands of men died in battle, and that six hundred virgin maidens were forcibly married to continue the tribe of Benjamin. What began with the rape of a woman concludes, in Judges 21, with the rape of six hundred daughters.

The narrator's ideology shows no compassion toward women. The nameless woman is not even given a chance to express herself. His will to destroy Benjamin's reputation and to justify the war that will lead toward a monarchy is so strong that it completely overshadows the woman's experience. This bias can't help but result in a negative image of the woman. However, a proactive reader can deconstruct the story to find a woman who is not a mere victim, but a survivor. In this way she could become a symbol of protest against sexual violence experienced by women.

Where Is God in This Biblical Account?

A reading of this narrative raises the question of sexual violence in the Bible – a kind of violence that unfortunately is still among us. God seems to be absent from the story. In the following chapter, however, the Lord is present, inciting the tribes to go to war against Benjamin (Judges 20:18-28). Which is better: the absence of God in chapter 19 or his military presence in chapter 20?

Perhaps God can be found in the woman's silence. The question of the presence/absence of God, amid suffering and death, marks several biblical texts, from psalms of supplication to the crucifixion of Jesus. Even today, men and women often wonder where God is when an innocent person is abused.

Cannibals in the Bible

Cannibalism is horrible, disgusting and monstrous. Settled nicely in the comfort of our own homes, we cannot imagine how it is possible to stoop that low. Yet famine and the approach of death can cause a person to do what is normally unthinkable. Killing and eating another human being was equally revolting in biblical times. And yet, we find biblical accounts that refer to acts of cannibalism.

Each passage dealing with cannibalism has common elements. There is always a siege. An enemy has surrounded a city, letting nothing in or out. Famine takes root and engenders all sorts of horrors. Curiously, the narratives specify that it is the children, the most vulnerable in society, who are eaten first.

The Siege of Samaria

During the second siege of Samaria by the Arameans, as described in the second book of Kings, a woman questions the king:

> [28]But then the king asked her, "What is your complaint?" She answered, "This woman said to me, 'Give up your son; we will eat him today, and we will eat my son tomorrow.' [29]So we cooked my son and ate him. The next day I said to her, 'Give up your son and we will

eat him.' But she has hidden her son." ³⁰When the king heard the words of the woman he tore his clothes—now since he was walking on the city wall, the people could see that he had sackcloth on his body underneath... (2 Kings 6:28-30)

Prediction of the Siege of Jerusalem

The prophet Jeremiah warns the people of Jerusalem that they must reform to avoid unbelievable catastrophes caused by their sinful ways. In chapter 19 he announces that the inhabitants of Jerusalem will experience a siege causing famine and destruction. And believe it or not, it is God who will guide the hands of their enemies to chastise his people:

⁹And I will make them eat the flesh of their sons and the flesh of their daughters, and all shall eat the flesh of their neighbours in the siege, and in the distress with which their enemies and those who seek their life afflict them. (Jeremiah 19:9)

This verse is based on a theme that appears in the books of Leviticus and Deuteronomy, indicating that Israel will be reduced to cannibalism in a siege if it does not obey the law of the Lord.

⁵³In the desperate straits to which the enemy siege reduces you, you will eat the fruit of your womb, the flesh of your own sons and daughters whom the Lord your God has given you. (Deuteronomy 28:53)

²⁷But if, despite this, you disobey me, and continue hostile to me, ²⁸I will continue hostile to you in fury; I

in turn will punish you myself sevenfold for your sins.
[29]You shall eat the flesh of your sons, and you shall eat
the flesh of your daughters. (Leviticus 26:27-29)

Each one of the excerpts relates that cannibalism occurs
during a famine caused by conflict. The famine is interpreted
as divine punishment.

The Siege of Jerusalem by the Romans

Flavius Josephus, a Jewish historian of the first century,
reports a narrative of cannibalism in 70 AD, during the siege
of Jerusalem by the Romans (see War of the Jews, Book VI).

It seems probable that acts of this nature did take place.
When the towns were besieged and there was no food left, there
was little choice for people but to eat their own. The texts relating these episodes convey the profound disgust of these acts.
It is intended that the reader be outraged, discouraging them
from doing such atrocities and encouraging them to follow in
the footsteps of the Lord.

Thirty-hour Famine

Famine is an unspeakable horror. It is a terrible reality that
people throughout the world do not have access to the food
they need to survive. These tragedies may seem distant from
our North American experience; in most developed countries,
there are places where you can get a free meal or free groceries
if you don't have enough to eat.

When I was working as a youth minister in a high school,
I discovered that teenagers react strongly to inequality and

injustice. They helped me to solidify the ethical calls of the gospel in my life. I had received information about a challenge to hold a "thirty-hour famine" to raise funds to fight hunger in the world. I never thought I could interest my teenage students from well-to-do families in fasting. Yet, when these students who were upset by the sight of children dying of starvation in Africa came to see me, I realized that the radical aspect of the project challenged them. In fact, the project was so popular, I had to limit the number of participants. Among various activities, during our 30 hours we reflected on poverty, using a text from Isaiah. As a result of this reading, the group decided to call itself "Thirsting for Justice." Reading the Bible – even the disturbing passages – should be an inspiration, a way for us to transform our world!

The Military Value of Drinking

During the judges' period in Israel, the Bible shows us men (and a woman, Deborah) called "judges" who ruled the tribes of Israel. This period is marked by wars between tribes and against neighbouring peoples. In chapter 7, it is Gideon who leads his people to war against the Midianites. This account demonstrates how he picked his soldiers.

> ²The Lord said to Gideon, "The troops with you are too many for me to give the Midianites into their hand. Israel would only take the credit away from me, saying, 'My own hand has delivered me.' ³Now therefore proclaim this in the hearing of the troops, 'Whoever is fearful and trembling, let him return home.'" Thus Gideon sifted them out; twenty-two thousand returned, and ten thousand remained.
>
> ⁴Then the Lord said to Gideon, "The troops are still too many; take them down to the water and I will sift them out for you there. When I say, 'This one shall go with you,' he shall go with you; and when I say, 'This one shall not go with you,' he shall not go." ⁵So he brought the troops down to the water; and the Lord said to Gideon, "All those who lap the water with their tongues, as a dog laps, you shall put to one side; all those who kneel down

to drink, putting their hands to their mouths, you shall put to the other side." ⁶The number of those that lapped was three hundred; but all the rest of the troops knelt down to drink water. ⁷Then the Lord said to Gideon, "With the three hundred that lapped I will deliver you, and give the Midianites into your hand. Let all the others go to their homes." (Judges 7:2-7)

For the narrator, the reduction of Gideon's army has a theological purpose. In reducing the army from 32,000 to 300 soldiers, the narrator shows that it is the glory of God and not human force that brings victory. Two criteria are used in choosing those fit to be soldiers. The first criterion is fear and trembling. It is understandable that a soldier who trembles and is afraid is probably not the best candidate. But this trembling can also be understood as a lack of faith or trust in the Lord. The second criterion is how men drink water. The men who take water into their hands and carry it to their mouth are selected. This appears to be a very arbitrary criterion. How can we make sense of it? Perhaps drinking with your hands, head held high, keeps you alert to see potential dangers. Another hypothesis is that lapping water is associated with animals, which would be pejorative. (The Bible likes to underline the difference between humans and animals. The story of Genesis gives humans the power to name and dominate animals.) Curiously, the majority of people lapped water directly with their mouth, like animals. If the only objective of this criterion was to select the smallest number of people possible, it made sense to eliminate the grand majority – those who lapped the water.

The rest of the story is equally interesting. Who will win the battle: Gideon and his 300 soldiers or the larger army of Midian?

[16]After he divided the three hundred men into three companies, and put trumpets into the hands of all of them, and empty jars, with torches inside the jars, [17]he said to them, "Look at me, and do the same; when I come to the outskirts of the camp, do as I do. [18]When I blow the trumpet, I and all who are with me, then you also blow the trumpets around the whole camp, and shout, 'For the Lord and for Gideon!'"

[19]So Gideon and the hundred who were with him came to the outskirts of the camp at the beginning of the middle watch, when they had just set the watch; and they blew the trumpets and smashed the jars that were in their hands. [20]So the three companies blew the trumpets and broke the jars, holding in their left hands the torches, and in their right hands the trumpets to blow; and they cried, "A sword for the Lord and for Gideon!" [21]Every man stood in his place all around the camp, and all the men in camp ran; they cried out and fled. [22]When they blew the three hundred trumpets, the Lord set every man's sword against his fellow and against all the army; and the army fled as far as Beth-shittah toward Zererah, as far as the border of Abel-meholah, by Tabbath. [23]And the men of Israel were called out from Naphtali and from Asher and from all Manasseh, and they pursued after the Midianites.

²⁴Then Gideon sent messengers throughout all the hill country of Ephraim, saying, "Come down against the Midianites and seize the waters against them, as far as Beth-barah, and also the Jordan." So all the men of Ephraim were called out, and they seized the waters as far as Beth-barah, and also the Jordan. ²⁵They captured the two captains of Midian, Oreb and Zeeb; they killed Oreb at the rock of Oreb, and Zeeb they killed at the wine press of Zeeb, as they pursued the Midianites. They brought the heads of Oreb and Zeeb to Gideon beyond the Jordan. (Judges 7:16-25)

What the narrator had predicted from the outset proves to be correct. The noise of the 300 horns sows terror among the enemies, who, in darkness and confusion, kill each other. In short, the Lord made sure that Gideon's army would succeed, even though it was smaller.

Water to the Rescue!

Have you noticed the importance of water in this story? First, it is associated with the criterion of soldier selection. Second, when the surviving Midianites fled, the first objective of Gideon's army was to secure the sources of water. In Israel, water is a scarce commodity, and the control of this resource is still a source of conflict. In this semi-desert region, rain is practically non-existent from April to September.

Water is an obvious geopolitical issue in the relationship between Israel and the Palestinians in the West Bank and Gaza today. Tensions originate, among other things, from a blatant disparity in water consumption between these two communities that must share the same sources of the water supply. The average consumption of an Israeli is four times that of a Palestinian.[4] This disparity stems from Israel's control of most of the water system in the occupied territories of Palestine.

The long-term prospects are alarming: water shortages will only increase, as resources are limited and demand increases. Several projects for the de-alienation of water are being studied, as well as a plan to create a canal that would make it possible to revive the Dead Sea with water from the Mediterranean. Ultimately, a more equitable sharing of water must be part of the Middle East peace negotiations.

---

4   According to an article in *Le Figaro*, March 20, 2013: http://www.lefigaro.fr/international/2013/03/20/01003-20130320ARTFIG00583-l-eau-enjeu-majeur-entre-israel-et-palestine.php.

Who Killed Goliath: David or Elhanan?

David and Goliath

The story of David's fight against Goliath is legendary. There is a saying: Might is not always right. That is the point of this narrative. Against all expectations, David, the young shepherd, kills Goliath, who is many times his weight and size.

Here is a brief review of the scene found in 1 Samuel 17:23-50. Goliath is described as a giant of "six cubits and a span" (1 Samuel 17:4) – about 2.90 metres. He is fitted with a copper chain coat weighing "5000 shekels," or 57 kilograms, and the iron blade of his spear weighs "600 shekels", more than 6 kilograms (1 Samuel 17:5, 7). Goliath, a member of the Philistine camp, challenges the Israeli army to find a man strong enough to fight a duel with him. The winner will determine the outcome of the battle between the two nations. This provocation is repeated for forty days, morning and evening, in the valley of Elath, the valley of the terebinths. In the end, it is David, a shepherd boy, who takes up Goliath's challenge. After declaring that he has the support of God, David throws a stone at the giant with his slingshot. The stone hits Goliath squarely on the forehead, causing him to fall to the ground. David then takes his sword and cuts off Goliath's head.

Elhanan and Goliath

This story is fundamental to understanding the popularity of David, who rose from humble shepherd to King of Israel. There is a second version of this story in the Bible.

[15]The Philistines went to war again with Israel, and David went down together with his servants. They fought against the Philistines, and David grew weary. [16]Ishbibenob, one of the descendants of the giants, whose spear weighed three hundred shekels of bronze, and who was fitted out with new weapons, said he would kill David. [17]But Abishai son of Zeruiah came to his aid, and attacked the Philistine and killed him. Then David's men swore to him, "You shall not go out with us to battle any longer, so that you do not quench the lamp of Israel"…

[19]Then there was another battle with the Philistines at Gob; and Elhanan son of Jaare-oregim, the Bethlehemite, killed Goliath the Gittite, the shaft of whose spear was like a weaver's beam… [22]These four were descended from the giants in Gath; they fell by the hands of David and his servants. (2 Samuel 21:15-17, 19, 22)

This is the very same Goliath, a Philistine from the city of Gath. But his opponent is named Elhanan, not David. The first verse of this story says that David was tired and that his servants were fighting the Philistines. Virtually nothing is known of Elhanan except that he is a servant of David and, like him, from Bethlehem.

Can We Reconcile These Traditions?

Who killed Goliath: David or Elhanan? The editor of the book of Chronicles wondered the same thing. To remove any confusion, he relates that Elhanan killed the brother of Goliath (1 Chronicles 20:5). It is possible that the story of the battle between David and Goliath was initially the work of one of David's servants, who amplified the feat and attributed it to his master, who was to become a great king. The narrative contains elements of legend that leave doubts about its historicity. Basically, the popularity of this narrative, which is one of the best known of the Old Testament stories, is due more to a fundamental message than to the truth of a historical event: brute strength and physical size do not always guarantee victory.

Did David Exist?

The narratives in the Bible tend to exaggerate the exploits of David, who became a king who was larger than life. We must remember that these texts were written hundreds of years after the events took place, when David was seen as the main representative of the monarchy. Since the exaggeration of events is so obvious, and since David is presented as such a legendary figure, many wonder if he actually existed.

Archaeology has given us something to think about. A stele (an upright sculptured tablet of stone) that was discovered in Tel-Dan in northern Israel in 1993 created a controversy because it mentioned the name of the house of David. Lines 7 to 9 of this stone read as follows:

7. [and I killed...] Ram son of [...]
8. The king of Israel, and I killed [...] yahu son of [...]
9. The house of David.

The text is incomplete. The heart of the disagreement lies in line 9, in a small series of letters: *bytdwd*, usually translated as "house of David." Do we have here an archaeological confirmation of David's reign?

Scholars are divided on this question. For Lemche, *bytdwd* should be translated as the name of a place. Bethdawid (House of David, or House of the Beloved) would be like Bethel (House of God) or Bethlehem (House of Bread). For this scholar, the stele of Tel-Dan does not prove anything about the existence of David.

For Finkelstein and Silberman, however, this line proves that David did exist. The fact that Judah is mentioned in reference to his royal house indicates that David's reputation was not merely a literary invention, embellished at a much later date. But for these authors, the kingdom of David was smaller than the descriptions in the biblical texts imply. The "kingdom" was disorganized, and its capital, Jerusalem, did not have much to do with the image in the Bible.

Other scholars, like Kitchen, believe that the stele of Tel-Dan proves that David is the founder of a major dynasty. Kitchen defends the version presented in the biblical text, relying on his interpretation of archaeological finds.

This overview of the controversies around the Tel-Dan stele shows us that behind the "objective" archaeological data (the stele) lies a great diversity in the understanding and meaning that can be given to this data, depending on the expert (or school) involved. As with ancient texts, archaeology relies on interpretation. And every interpretation is based on subjectivity, relying on the assumptions of the researchers. Each of the three experts looked at the same object and came up with different conclusions, because they see it in light of their own presuppositions.

Laughing at a Prophet's Baldness

My friends and family know I've been losing my hair since I was eighteen. I'm gradually going bald! A few people tease me about that, but my self-esteem is not based on my physical appearance. Why am I talking about my hair loss? Because the baldness of a biblical prophet is at the source of a bizarre narrative.

In the books of Kings, Elisha succeeds the prophet Elijah. Elisha is said to be a man of God, capable of performing powerful feats. But apparently, he had a problem. Elisha was bald and did not like hearing about it. Here's what happened when some young boys decided to laugh at him.

> [23]He went up from there to Bethel; and while he was going up on the way, some small boys came out of the city and jeered at him, saying, "Go away, baldhead! Go away, baldhead!" [24]When he turned around and saw them, he cursed them in the name of the Lord. Then two she-bears came out of the woods and mauled forty-two of the boys. (2 Kings 2:23-24)

Okay, the boys should not have laughed at the prophet, but the punishment seems disproportionate to the crime. Is this proper behaviour for a prophet? Isn't his reaction excessive? The text implies that the arrival of the bears and the death of forty-two children are consequences of the curse Elisha spoke. How can one make sense of this strange tale?

Before going any further, we must understand that the narrative is undoubtedly not historical. Two years ago, I spent time in a part of Canada where there is a large bear population. Occasionally, they attack people, but they never go so far as to kill forty-two at once! How was it that no one came to the children's defence? Why didn't most of the children have time to escape when two or three of their friends were being attacked? The scene is not very plausible.

Most contemporary readers react by protesting against the prophet's gesture and against the image of God presented in the story. With good reason, we can oppose this text by asserting that, since it was written, our image of God has changed drastically.

Getting Back to Context

At the time the narrative was written, its meaning was obvious to the reader. The beginning of the chapter from which this story is drawn evokes the passage of Elijah and the transmission of his powers to his disciple Elisha. The Bible gives evidence that some people disagreed with this succession. The narrative in question put an end to the disputes. If those who tease Elisha are given such treatment, imagine what would happen to those who would oppose him!

The verses just before this story (19-22) demonstrate the power of Elisha, who, through a special blessing, provided the city of Jericho with pure water. Similarly, in the story of the bald prophet, the book of Kings shows that the word of Elisha is powerful – powerful enough to lead to the deaths of forty-two children.

Appearance and Self-Esteem

Elisha was hurt by the taunts about his baldness. Bodily appearance seemed to be so important to him, he could not handle the children's laughter. In our culture, physical appearance is probably as important as it was in biblical times, if not more so. While working in a high school, I quickly saw that those who do not meet the usual criteria of beauty are quickly rejected by others. Adolescents, in general, are very sensitive to the importance of denouncing racism or homophobia, but strangely, they seem reluctant to react against the exclusion of people who are overweight, for example. I never understood girls who applied makeup every day before coming to school when they are naturally very beautiful. Imagine – some of them even use face creams to fight wrinkles!

We find the same dilemma in today's adult world: Botox, plastic surgery, skin care products, makeup, hair removal, hair implants, etc. Following fashion trends is very expensive. And yet, does all this improve our self-esteem? I doubt it. Even after all possible and unimaginable modifications, when we look at ourselves in the mirror, it is not how closely we adhere to accepted standards of beauty that makes us ready to love ourselves. Appearance is only one aspect of a person. To really love one's self is the work of a lifetime. When Jesus is asked what is the greatest commandment, he replies that, on the one hand, we must love God, and on the other hand, we must love our neighbour as ourselves (Matthew 22:37-40). Loving ourselves presupposes the ability to love one another. We need to have good self-esteem to love our neighbour. Working with teenagers, I became aware of how self-esteem is a crucial factor in a person's development.

Punishing His People and Torturing Prostitutes

In this disconcerting story, the prophet Ezekiel tells a symbolic tale of two sisters: Ohola represents the kingdom of Samaria, and Oholiba, the kingdom of Jerusalem. Ohola is sexually abused and killed by her people. The following is Oholiba's story:

> [19]Yet she increased her whorings, remembering the days of her youth, when she played the whore in the land of Egypt [20]and lusted after her paramours there, whose members were like those of donkeys, and whose emission was like that of stallions. [21]Thus you longed for the lewdness of your youth, when the Egyptians fondled your bosom and caressed your young breasts.

> [22]Therefore, O Oholibah, thus says the Lord God: I will rouse against you your lovers from whom you turned in disgust, and I will bring them against you from every side: [23]the Babylonians and all the Chaldeans, Pekod and Shoa and Koa, and all the Assyrians with them, handsome young men, governors and commanders all of them, officers and warriors, all of them riding on horses. [24]They shall come against you from the north with chariots and wagons and a host of peoples; they shall set themselves against you on every side with

buckler, shield, and helmet, and I will commit the judgment to them, and they shall judge you according to their ordinances. [25]I will direct my indignation against you, in order that they may deal with you in fury. They shall cut off your nose and your ears, and your survivors shall fall by the sword. They shall seize your sons and your daughters, and your survivors shall be devoured by fire. [26]They shall also strip you of your clothes and take away your fine jewels. [27]So I will put an end to your lewdness and your whoring brought from the land of Egypt; you shall not long for them, or remember Egypt any more. [28]For thus says the Lord God: I will deliver you into the hands of those whom you hate, into the hands of those from whom you turned in disgust; [29]and they shall deal with you in hatred, and take away all the fruit of your labour, and leave you naked and bare, and the nakedness of your whorings shall be exposed. Your lewdness and your whorings [30]have brought this upon you, because you played the whore with the nations, and polluted yourself with their idols. [31]You have gone the way of your sister; therefore I will give her cup into your hand. [32]Thus says the Lord God:

You shall drink your sister's cup, deep and wide; you shall be scorned and derided, it holds so much. [33]You shall be filled with drunkenness and sorrow. A cup of horror and desolation is the cup of your sister Samaria; [34]you shall drink it and drain it out, and gnaw its sherds, and tear out your breasts; for I have spoken, says the

Lord God. [35]Therefore thus says the Lord God: Because you have forgotten me and cast me behind your back, therefore bear the consequences of your lewdness and whorings…

[46]For thus says the Lord God: Bring up an assembly against them, and make them an object of terror and of plunder. [47]The assembly shall stone them and with their swords they shall cut them down; they shall kill their sons and their daughters, and burn up their houses. [48]Thus will I put an end to lewdness in the land, so that all women may take warning and not commit lewdness as you have done. [49]They shall repay you for your lewdness, and you shall bear the penalty for your sinful idolatry; and you shall know that I am the Lord God. (Ezekiel 23:19-35, 46-49)

It was probably because of tales like this one that the Church did not recommend that the faithful read the Bible in the past. A film based on this excerpt would most certainly be rated "Restricted"!

Putting It in Context

The chosen people were divided in two: to the north, a great kingdom called Israel, with Samaria as its capital; to the south, a smaller kingdom called Judah, whose capital was Jerusalem. History tells us that the kingdom of Israel was destroyed by the Assyrians in 722 BC. A large part of the population took refuge in the south, in the kingdom of Judah, which fell into the hands of the Babylonians in 587 BC. Ezekiel lived at the time of the destruction of Jerusalem by Babylon. Faced with such devastation, the survivors ask why the Lord let his people be crushed. Ezekiel responds that the Israelites were the cause of their own misfortune. Since they first knew the Lord, while living in Egypt, they have continued to worship other gods. Ezekiel uses the metaphor of adultery to explain the infidelity of his people. This narrative shows that it was God's vengeance that allowed his people to be destroyed at the hands of other nations, comparing Israel with an unfaithful wife.

Prostitutes and Jerusalem Share a Similar Fate

Here is a summary of Oholiba's misfortunes: she is raped by many men, they cut off her nose and ears, her children are burned, she is stoned, they steal her belongings, expose her naked body, force her to mutilate her own breasts, and finally kill her with a sword. This explicit language describes two horrors to which the Hebrew people were subjected. On the one hand, there is the fate of the kingdom of Judah and its inhabitants, after the destruction of Jerusalem by Babylon. All the biblical texts referring to this event describe it with unprecedented violence. Survivors must have witnessed barbaric scenes they could never have imagined. On the other hand, the narrative describes the fate of prostitutes and women who committed adultery at that time. For the metaphor to be effective and bring home the message, the prophet had to translate his theological message into imagery that his readers knew and understood all too well. These scenes of torture shock us today, but the first readers were used to seeing such scenes of violence involving women who broke sexual taboos.

What to Do with Such a Violent Text?

As a modern reader, I find this narrative difficult to accept. It goes against my understanding of God, and the treatment of women is shocking. In making a parallel to today, many people have abandoned the God of the Bible. Did they have the same fate as Oholiba? No! The Bible contains many images of God. We cannot simply superimpose them, since some of them are diametrically opposed to each other. I have to choose from among these biblical proposals. As a Christian, I have decided to follow Jesus and focus on the image of God he presents to us: that of a parent who loves and listens to his children. Yet this horrible story from Ezekiel is not to be hidden away. We can read it. We can talk about it. But we must analyze the situation and reject the violence inherent in certain biblical texts.

In the past, Christians justified the violence of their crusades and executions of the Inquisition by the violence found in the Bible. We have a responsibility to learn how to read these texts and how to interpret them using our good judgment.

Divine Punishment and Manure

The following text, from the prophet Malachi, uses disgusting images to pass on an important message. The prophets of the Bible are not always politically correct.

> ²If you will not listen, if you will not lay it to heart to give glory to my name, says the Lord of hosts, then I will send the curse on you and I will curse your blessings; indeed I have already cursed them, because you do not lay it to heart. ³I will rebuke your offspring, and spread dung on your faces, the dung of your offerings, and I will put you out of my presence. ⁴Know, then, that I have sent this command to you, that my covenant with Levi may hold, says the Lord of hosts. (Malachi 2:2-4)

A Dubious Pedagogy

The pedagogy the Lord uses is more than a little dubious. It reminds me of dog owners who house train their pets by forcing their muzzles into their own excrement. This strategy of intimidation, humiliation and vulgarity does not correspond to the usual image of God in the Bible.

You Priests Are Full of…

This passage from the book of Malachi targets Jewish priests using a rather direct approach. The prophet contrasts the priests of his time with Levi, recognized as the founder of the priestly caste. The covenant between the Lord and Levi was marked by "life and well-being" (Malachi 2:5). Levi's teaching was completely in union with the Lord. Unfortunately, some of his successors turned their backs on the Lord and dragged the people away from the straight and narrow path.

As a curse, the Lord throws animal feces into the priests' faces. The contrast between the ritual purity demanded of priests and the manure is striking. Furthermore, the Lord chooses carefully the excrement used to defile them. He takes the dung from the very animals the priests offered him as a sacrifice. This detail is beyond unusual. Prophets like Malachi used very harsh words about the sacrifices offered to the Lord. In the eyes of the prophets, these sacrifices were utterly useless if the priests ignored the principles of law and justice: "For I desire steadfast love and not sacrifice, the knowledge of God rather than burnt offerings" (Hosea 6:6). Jesus reiterates these vibrant words of Hosea when speaking against sacrifices in Matthew 9:13. The four gospels recount that Jesus strongly disputed these practices in the Temple, the heart of the sacrificial system. This gesture eventually led to his condemnation and execution by the religious authorities and politicians of his time.

The Priests of Today

It would be simple-minded to use this text as an excuse for throwing dung in the faces of today's priests. There is a big difference between the priests of the Old Testament and the priests of the modern Church. These ministers of the Church were first called "presbyters" in the New Testament. These officials did not offer sacrifices, like Jewish priests did. The term "priest" in English comes from the word "presbyter," which has been distorted by passing through Latin. As they do not exercise the same functions, Christian priests have little connection with Jewish priests.

Still, I think there is a great deal of thought to be given to how responsibilities are shared in the Church. This text of the prophet Malachi challenges today's Church and invites it to face the task of fulfilling its mission. "But you have turned aside from the way; you have caused many to stumble by your instruction" (Malachi 2:8). What is the result of the preaching of our priests? Does it cause scandal, exclusion or indifference?

The current crisis in the Catholic Church may be transformed into a positive opportunity. If the Church is the people of God, it is up to each and every one of us to commit ourselves to transform it from within and foster a renewal. Let us hope that the call of the Lord, as transmitted by Malachi, is a wake-up call.

Ah! The Joy of Crushing the Heads of Babies!

Psalms are prayers, poems and songs driven by vivid human emotions. Here is a psalm containing a disturbing prayer.

¹By the rivers of Babylon—
    there we sat down and there we wept
    when we remembered Zion.
²On the willows there
    we hung up our harps.
³For there our captors
    asked us for songs,
and our tormentors asked for mirth, saying,
    "Sing us one of the songs of Zion!"

⁴How could we sing the Lord's song
    in a foreign land?
⁵If I forget you, O Jerusalem,
    let my right hand wither!
⁶Let my tongue cling to the roof of my mouth,
    if I do not remember you,
if I do not set Jerusalem
    above my highest joy.

⁷Remember, O Lord, against the Edomites
    the day of Jerusalem's fall,
how they said, "Tear it down! Tear it down!
    Down to its foundations!"

⁸O daughter Babylon, you devastator!
    Happy shall they be who pay you back
    what you have done to us!
⁹Happy shall they be who take your little ones
    and dash them against the rock! (Psalm 137)

This psalm refers to the destruction of Jerusalem in 587 BC, and to the exile that followed. The psalmist presents himself as one who is exiled to the banks of the rivers of Babylon. The beginning of the text contrasts the joyful tunes requested by the Babylonians and the psalmist's emotions of profound sadness and melancholy. After a passage devoted to the memory of Jerusalem, the psalm turns its attention to the Edomites, a neighbouring nation of Israel that joined the Babylonians when the city was plundered (Obadiah 11). The final verses directly accuse the Babylonians of extreme cruelty. At that time, the massacre of babies was a common practice during the looting of a conquered city. It was both a symbolic and a very real way of destroying the future of a people. It can be assumed that the inhabitants of Jerusalem saw their own children suffer this fate. This is why, ironically, the songs of joy that the Babylonians demanded evoke the psalmist's macabre bliss: Happy is he who will seize Babylonian babies and do to them what they did to us!

Praying with Feeling

I confess that I love reading this psalm. It is not that I am sadistic: I like to read it because it encourages me to pray with authentic emotions. In the Catholic tradition, prayer is often so ritualized that it has little to do with real emotions. The reading of the psalms teaches me that when we are angry, we do not have to pretend that everything is beautiful, or that we live in the best of all possible worlds. When I am angry, I can pray without repressing my feelings. I even have the right to be angry with God! Psalm 22, which Jesus quotes on the cross, asks, "My God, my God, why have you forsaken me?" – showing paradoxically that we can offer to God our feeling of being abandoned by him.

I have often heard emotionally charged alleluias proclaimed monotonously. The psalms can enable us to put the whole range of human emotions into words and toss them to God. We should try to include some of these real emotions in our liturgies!

Psalm 137 is often recited during church celebrations, but its last verse is always skipped over, on the pretext that including it would require too much explanation. It is true that these verses demand clarification, but once these clarifications are made, the end of the psalm offers us the opportunity to learn to pray with deep emotions.

Is an Evil Man Better than a Good Woman?

Like most Christians, when I read the Bible, I try to be a conciliatory reader; I try to understand the narrator's point of view. But in this case, forget it! This quote from Sirach is completely sexist. What can we do with a biblical text like this? Instead of pretending that it does not exist, here is a reflection on this text which might help us understand what the Bible is about and how to interpret it today.

A Patriarchal Context

Sirach is a biblical book written by Jesus Ben Sira, between 200 and 175 BC, a time when Greek wisdom was questioning the traditional way of living in Palestine. It is in this context that Ben Sira writes to defend the cultural, religious and social heritage of Israel. Sirach is thus the work of a conservative who is trying to save what he considers essential in his cultural tradition when it is faced with new tendencies. The patriarchal culture is the one element he wants to preserve at all costs.

The Literary Context

When we interpret it literally, this passage is very clear: women are so bad that a wicked man is better than a good woman. The previous verses portray a girl who might be a cause of worry for her father. She can lose her virginity, have difficulty finding a husband, be hated by her husband, be unfaithful, be sterile, and so on. It is to this girl, a source of potential shame for her father, that this passage is addressed:

> [12]Do not let her parade her beauty before any man, or spend her time among married women; [13]for from garments comes the moth, and from a woman comes woman's wickedness. [14]Better is the wickedness of a man than a woman who does good; it is woman who brings shame and disgrace. (Sirach 42:12-14)

Not only does the text put down women in general, but it also recommends that girls avoid seeking advice from other women, to avoid being influenced by their wayward thoughts. Basically, it is a strategy to impose a macho vision of social relations and to remove girls from contact with potentially subversive women.

How awful! My personal values are completely at odds with the message this text conveys. Does a Christian have the right to be critical of a misogynist passage from the Bible?

Love as an Interpretive Criteria

To judge a biblical interpretation, we can examine how effective it is. Does it justify violence? Does it produce good fruit? In light of Augustine's precept to "Love and do what you want," love becomes the hermeneutic key to judging the value of an interpretation. To read this passage literally and accept it obediently leads to the alienation of half of humanity. This goes against the principle of Augustine – and the gospel.

Where Is God in All This?

Another way of thinking is to ask where God is in the text. It is impossible for me to say that this text is automatically the word of God. At best, perhaps God is present in the silence of the girl to whom this advice is addressed. She is not given the chance to speak up in such a male-oriented text. In light of many other biblical texts that show God on the side of the excluded, perhaps God is in solidarity with women, whose goodness is denied by this short excerpt.

Perhaps God is in the glimmer of hope transmitted by this passage. If Ben Sira advises the girl not to mingle with other women, it is probably because they represented an element of resistance to the patriarchal culture. These women represent hope: a possible subversion before the macho attitude of the text.

Resisting Biblical Sexism

My personal reader response to this text can be positive. Faced with a sexist text, I can only resist and challenge the point of view it presents. The result of my reading is probably the opposite of what the author intended. The more I read and meditate on it, the more I wish to fight for the equality of women and men. Basically, my experience of reading this text gives a very positive result, since it allows me to distance myself from the patriarchal culture that gave birth to it. It is therefore an outlet for me to act with clearheadedness in my own society.

According to the National Sexual Violence Resource Center in the US, one in five women and one in 71 men will be raped. Rape is the most underreported crime: 63% of sexual assaults are not reported to police.[5] While the numbers can never be 100% accurate, we can make a few key generalizations: sexual assault is far more common than most people suspect; relatively few incidents of sexual assault are reported to the police; and young and other vulnerable women are most likely to be sexually abused. We still have a long way to go! Why are women still harassed and assaulted, when we have equality of the sexes in other areas of life? Unfortunately, the mentality of many men belongs to the era of Ben Sira. For me, reading the Bible today means taking up these sexist passages and thinking about them in a way that enables us to deconstruct this misogynistic culture.

---

5   http://www.nsvrc.org

How to Find Unicorns in the Bible

It is well known that social networks are a fertile breeding ground for urban legends. So the first time I saw an image ridiculing the Bible because it speaks of unicorns, I did not make a big deal of it. And when a former student approached me and asked me if there were unicorns in the Bible, I said no. In fact, I had read the Bible from cover to cover, and I did not remember seeing anything about this mythical animal. But it turns out there *are* unicorns in the Bible … it all depends on the translation you use.

I had not seen the passages about unicorns because the translations I use come from the Hebrew text of the Old Testament. To find unicorns in the Bible, you need the first Greek translation, called the Septuagint. The translators ran into difficulty when they came upon the Hebrew word *reem*. They didn't know which animal this word referred to, so they translated it into Greek as *monoceros* (one horn). When Jerome translated the Bible into Latin, he based his work on the Septuagint, translating *monoceros* as *unicornis*, or "unicorn."

Therefore, if we read the Bible in certain translations, such as the King James Version, we find a unicorn in the book of Job and in the Psalms:

⁹Will the unicorn be willing to serve thee, or abide by thy crib? ¹⁰Canst thou bind the unicorn with his band in the furrow? or will he harrow the valleys after thee? (Job 39:9-10 KJV)

⁵The voice of the Lord breaketh the cedars;
yea, the Lord breaketh the cedars of Lebanon.
⁶He maketh them also to skip like a calf;
Lebanon and Sirion like a young unicorn.
(Psalm 29:5-6 KJV)

In fact, if you are looking for unicorns in the Septuagint (or King James Version), you will find them in the following places: Psalm 22:21, Psalm 29:6, Psalm 92:10, Isaiah 34:7, Job 39:9-10, Numbers 23:22, Numbers 24:8 and Deuteronomy 33:17.

As a result of this unfortunate translation error, for centuries Christendom didn't doubt the existence of unicorns. Why would they? After all, according to the Bible, these creatures existed. It was not understood until much later that the biblical *reem* was an animal with no supernatural powers. It is now assumed that it was a kind of wild bull.

A Theological Image

In many of these passages, the *reem* (unicorn/wild bull) is a symbol for God's power of salvation. Also, in the culture of the ancient Near East, wild bulls were symbols of strength and sexual power. Bull horns were often used in representing the gods or as a royal symbol. Knowing this, we can understand using the horn of a wild bull, badly translated as a unicorn, to represent the power of God (Psalm 22:21 and Numbers 23:22).

The symbol of the power of God who freed his people from Egypt resembled that of a wild bull … and not that of a unicorn.

Translating Is Betraying!

The Bible contains many supernatural and wonder-filled elements, but the unicorn is not one of them. This error of translation shows us that the millennia that separate us from the time when these texts were written cannot be bridged too quickly. Biblical texts were written in another language and culture, and we must go through translation to access them, unless we learn ancient Greek and Hebrew. As the Italian maxim says, *Traduttore, traditore!* – "Translating is betraying." Every translation, even at its best, is imperfect, and cannot be otherwise. The translator of Sirach warns the reader about this:

> You are invited therefore to read it with goodwill and attention, and to be indulgent in cases where, despite our diligent labour in translating, we may seem to have rendered some phrases imperfectly. For what was originally expressed in Hebrew does not have exactly the same meaning when translated into another language. Not only this book, but even the Law itself, the Prophecies, and the rest of the books differ quite a bit from the original. (Sirach, Prologue 15-25)

It is possible to read and understand the Bible today, but we should never forget that these texts were written in other languages and that they come from a culture that is very different from our own. Before we grasp what the text can mean for us today, we must try to understand what the original text meant.

The New Testament

Saint Joseph's Two Fathers

Do you know Jesus' grandparents? Two biblical texts speak about them: the Gospels of Luke and Matthew. But they give different names for Joseph's father: Heli and Jacob. Who is right? Did Joseph have two fathers?

The Texts

Matthew opens his gospel with a genealogy that extends from Abraham to Jesus, through David. In verse 16 we read, "Jacob the father of Joseph the husband of Mary, of whom Jesus was born, who is called the Messiah." Luke places the genealogy of Jesus just before the beginning of his public ministry. This begins with the name of Jesus and goes back in time to Adam. "Jesus was about thirty years old when he began his work. He was the son (as was thought) of Joseph son of Heli" (Luke 3:23).

What can we do with these two statements? Is Joseph's father called Jacob, as Matthew states, or Heli, as Luke reports? The opponents of a literal reading of the Bible have been busy trying to answer this question. They have found some creative answers.

The Father of Mary?

The first hypothesis is that one of the two genealogies is that of Mary, not Joseph. Jacob would be Joseph's father, and Heli, Mary's father. This position is difficult to sustain, since the two texts clearly state that it is the genealogy of Jesus by Joseph and not by Mary. In any case, biblical genealogies always follow the father's line. Note that tradition gives the name of Joachim to Mary's father, based on the Infancy Gospel of James, a popular apocryphal gospel from the second century.

Two Fathers?

To support a literal interpretation of the genealogies of Matthew and Luke, Julius Africanus proposed an original solution in the third century by invoking the law of the levirate. If a married man died childless, his next of kin should marry his widow, and the children born of that marriage should bear the name of the deceased. For him, Jacob and Heli were brothers. Jacob would have been the biological father of Joseph, and Heli his father by adoption. This hypothesis seems unlikely, since no biblical text supports it.

Two Names for One Father

In our contemporary culture, truth is almost always confused with historical facts. For us, what is true is what really happened. But in the cultures of antiquity, this distinction does not rigorously exist. Symbolic elements may well mingle with historical data, while still being considered true. Matthew and Luke did not have access to a list of ancestors from Adam to Jesus. They composed genealogies whose objective was to describe who Jesus was by attributing ancestors to him. Also, the two lists differ on all the names between David and Jesus. These two genealogies do not have a historical objective, but rather have a theological purpose.

So Joseph certainly had one father. His name remains uncertain; Luke calls him Heli and Matthew calls him Jacob. But the two names probably refer to the same person.

Absent Father, Missed Son?

Today, with so many reconstituted families with countless variations, including open relationships and artificial insemination, it becomes more and more difficult to build family trees. A child may well have two fathers, if his biological father is not his mother's spouse. A child raised by a gay couple ends up in the same situation. Paternity evolves and changes.

Other children have no father: perhaps he has died or is estranged from the family, or he never recognized the child as his own. A child of an absent father might spend the rest of his life seeking love and recognition from a father figure. Could Jesus' deep intimacy with God be due to the absence of a father in his daily life? We don't know. Apart from the stories of Jesus' childhood and two references to Jesus as the son of Joseph (Luke 4:22 and John 1:45), Joseph is not mentioned anywhere else in the New Testament.

Not being a psychologist, I am not qualified to talk about the importance of a father in a child's development. But my intuition tells me that everyone benefits from knowing their origins. One of the most obvious ways to answer the question

"Who am I?" is to say that I am the child of my parents, and I belong to such-and-such a family. I am registered with them in the history of a people and of humanity. Genealogical landmarks help define our personal identity.

Was Jesus Against Public Prayer?

We tend to forget this point, but Jesus was neither Christian nor Catholic. He was not ordained and did not preside at mass, baptisms or funerals. He was a secular Jew, and his way of praying was not necessarily ours. At the heart of the Sermon on the Mount, Matthew's Gospel reports Jesus' shocking words about prayer. In particular, he was against praying in public to attract attention.

> [5]"And whenever you pray, do not be like the hypocrites; for they love to stand and pray in the synagogues and at the street corners, so that they may be seen by others. Truly I tell you, they have received their reward. [6]But whenever you pray, go into your room and shut the door and pray to your Father who is in secret; and your Father who sees in secret will reward you.

> [7]"When you are praying, do not heap up empty phrases as the Gentiles do; for they think that they will be heard because of their many words. [8]Do not be like them, for your Father knows what you need before you ask him.

> [9]"Pray then in this way: Our Father in heaven, hallowed be your name. [10]Your kingdom come. Your will be done, on earth as it is in heaven. [11]Give us this day our daily bread. [12]And forgive us our debts, as we also have for-

given our debtors. [13]And do not bring us to the time of trial, but rescue us from the evil one." (Matthew 6:5-13)

Before teaching the disciples the Our Father, Jesus encouraged them to pray authentically, from the heart. He paints a portrait of someone who prays hypocritically, who wants to be seen praying, repeating formulas, thinking that God will magically grant whatever he asks. Jesus proclaims that God already knows what we need. Then he gives an example of prayer by reciting the Our Father. When he invites us to pray in this way, there are two possible interpretations: he wants us to repeat these same words, or he encourages us to pray in a personal and creative way, drawing inspiration from his words without merely repeating them.

"Our Father in Heaven"

One of the distinctive elements of Jesus' spirituality is that we should relate to God as a child addresses a loving father. This Father is the same for all of us – it is *our* Father. In praying in this way, we recognize that our relationship with God is not individual. The prayer is on behalf of a community of people who see themselves as sons and daughters of God.

"Hallowed be thy name."

Sanctifying God or God's name is a classic expression that means recognizing God's active presence. This expression invites us to seek the presence of God in our life and in our world.

"Your kingdom come. Your will be done..."

In this request we ask God to manifest his will. Of course, God's will concerns us. Jesus invites us to participate in building a world of justice and peace, which he calls "the kingdom of God." How can we participate in building the kingdom of God? How do we discern God's will?

"Give us this day our daily bread."

In Jesus' time, there were fewer food choices. Bread was the basic element. Jesus invites us to ask God to respond to our most concrete needs, day by day, as he did with the Hebrew people in the desert by giving them manna when they were hungry (Exodus 16). What do we need to live? What are our greatest desires? Can God help us achieve them?

"And forgive us our debts…"

The biblical text literally speaks of paying off financial debts. In the society of that time, debts were a matter of life or death. Those who could not pay their debts were imprisoned, and sometimes their entire family was enslaved. To pay the debt of such a person was, in a way, to restore his freedom and his life. In praying with these words, we are asking God to cancel the debts we owe him, similar to a legal pardon. These debts represent our wrongs, our sins.

"And lead us not into temptation…"

In the culture of the New Testament, it is not God who is at the origin of the misfortunes that afflict us, but rather the Tempter, Satan. The Our Father ends with a request to God to actively intervene to free us from the forces of evil.

Praying Today

In the first part of Matthew's text, Jesus criticizes the way people prayed in his time. We might ask ourselves what types of prayer would be considered hypocritical today. Ostentatious prayers, whose purpose is to showcase us, seem to be the most obvious answer. Since prayer is such a personal act, our goal should never be to pray as others would like us to pray, but rather to aim for authenticity in our prayer.

There are many ways to pray: asking for something, saying formal prayers, meditation, praise, singing, and more. How do you pray? What is prayer for you? My prayer is nourished by the songs of Taizé, an ecumenical community based in France. This form of prayer invites us to meditate by singing brief songs over and over. These days, I have been exploring other ways of praying to deepen my spiritual life. For example, since I run about 1,000 kilometres a year, I use this time to get in touch with the natural world that surrounds me. There is no better way to discover an artist than by contemplating what they have created. I like to stop from time to time, be silent and concentrate on my breathing. In the creation story in the book of Genesis, it is God who gives life to humankind through his breath. Every breath I take can be an opportunity to make myself aware of this breath, a gift from God. Another example: even worldly activities such as a day at the spa can be an expression of our spirituality. First, rest allows me to get back in touch with myself. Then the silence of the spa allows me to pray and meditate: when I am there, time stops and I open myself to prayer.

This is my personal way of praying. What is yours?

Hating Relatives to Follow Jesus

Some biblical passages are difficult to interpret. In the following example, Jesus says something that, fortunately, Christians do not take literally.

> [25]Now large crowds were travelling with him; and he turned and said to them, [26]"Whoever comes to me and does not hate father and mother, wife and children, brothers and sisters, yes, and even life itself, cannot be my disciple. [27]Whoever does not carry the cross and follow me cannot be my disciple." (Luke 14:25-27)

In some translations, this passage is taken as Jesus simply asking his disciples to prefer him over their family members. Disciples must leave everything, because following him requires renunciation and suffering. This interpretation is acceptable, but in verse 26, the Greek text of the gospel manuscripts according to Luke uses the verb *miso*, which translates literally as the verb "hate." In the NRSV translation, Jesus asks his future disciples to hate their father, mother, wife, children, brothers, sisters and even their own lives! This is a far cry from the famous "Love one another"!

This recommendation probably stems from the many family conflicts experienced by disciples who decided to follow Jesus. Moreover, the gospels mention the sharp tension that existed between Jesus and his own family. Mark 3:20-35, for example, describes how the mother and brothers of Jesus wanted to grab hold of him because they believed he had "lost his head." Warned of their presence, Jesus denied his family in front of those present, asserting that his true family was made up of "whoever does the will of God." In a rural society like that of Galilee, it was not acceptable to leave one's family and village. Jesus and his disciples upset the established order, leaving their loved ones behind. It was not only a question of giving up what they had, but of freeing themselves from their family responsibilities. The departure of the men who followed Jesus would have had negative repercussions on the people who depended on them. They had to make heartbreaking choices that were unacceptable to the members of the families with whom they broke ties, as if they hated them.

Hating Family

We do not need to take these verses literally. We can choose to put Jesus first without necessarily hating our family. Besides, I like my family, and this message of Jesus will not make me hate them. On the other hand, at certain moments in life we do need to make personal choices and distance ourselves from family demands. For example, when teenagers are becoming adults, they must gradually learn to make their own choices. While working in a high school, I discovered that a large proportion of teens consider themselves to be in conflict with their parents. I think that's normal. Teens must learn to make their own choices and parents must learn to give them some independence. Once teens become adults, they can build a more cordial relationship with their parents. I have been there. As a teenager, I was rude and insulting to my mother. It seemed to me that I had to do this to assert myself and become the person I wanted to be. I am happy to say that I have a very good relationship with my mother now that we communicate as equals, as adults.

The Most Beautiful Story of the Bible Almost Did Not Make It In

Here, in my opinion, is the most beautiful biblical text found in this collection of strange tales. It presents an image of Jesus whose compassion and forgiveness are not limited by the Law. I find it particularly interesting because the inclusion of this text in the Bible was not a given. A look at the origins of the following narrative will give us the opportunity to take a little detour to better understand the way the gospels were put together.

³The scribes and the Pharisees brought a woman who had been caught in adultery; and making her stand before all of them, ⁴they said to him, "Teacher, this woman was caught in the very act of committing adultery. ⁵Now in the law Moses commanded us to stone such women. Now what do you say?" ⁶They said this to test him, so that they might have some charge to bring against him. Jesus bent down and wrote with his finger on the ground. ⁷When they kept on questioning him, he straightened up and said to them, "Let anyone among you who is without sin be the first to throw a stone at her." ⁸And once again he bent down and wrote on the ground. ⁹When they heard it, they went away, one by

one, beginning with the elders; and Jesus was left alone with the woman standing before him. [10]Jesus straightened up and said to her, "Woman, where are they? Has no one condemned you?" [11]She said, "No one, sir." And Jesus said, "Neither do I condemn you. Go your way, and from now on do not sin again." (John 8:3-11)

This story as such does not say anything particularly unusual. And it is one of the best-loved texts of the New Testament. But is it authentic? Should it be in the Bible?

Compare the Manuscripts!

Do you know where the texts in the Bible come from? They are translations into English from Greek (New Testament) and Hebrew (Old Testament). And where do the Greek and Hebrew texts come from? As with all texts from antiquity, no original manuscripts exist. Take the case of the Gospel according to John. The earliest manuscript we have dates from around 125 AD. Most scholars agree that the final phase of the writing of this gospel was around 90 AD. After this date, the manuscripts were recopied by hand for distribution. This is why today, we do not have the original copy of John, but several thousand manuscripts exist in Greek. We also have translations in ancient languages, such as Latin and Syriac. Besides the manuscripts, many of the Fathers of the Church cite the Gospel of John in their own writing. There are discrepancies between these manuscripts. What do we do when we find several versions of the same verse? Which is the "correct" text of the Gospel according to John?

Welcome to the World of Textual Criticism!

Experts devote their lives to comparing and evaluating manuscripts, trying to figure out which version is closest to the original text. Their discipline is "textual criticism." The fruit of their work produces a text in Greek or Hebrew that is intended to be a reconstruction of the original text, as well as several footnotes indicating where various manuscripts differ.

The Case of the Adulterous Woman

The story of the adulterous woman is absent from the two most important New Testament manuscripts: the Codex Vaticanus and the Codex Sinaiticus. These manuscripts date from the middle of the fourth century. They are the oldest codexes, grouping together the entire New Testament as we know it. As in the case of the Vaticanus and Sinaiticus codexes, most ancient manuscripts do not contain the narrative of the adulterous woman, which appears only in certain manuscripts dating from the fifth century and beyond. Also, the manuscripts in which this story is written situate it in various places in the Bible: instead of being in John 8, some place it later, in chapter 21. Others situate it at the end of chapter 24 of the Gospel of Luke. This last choice is not without reason, since it is true that the literary style of this narrative is closer to that of Luke than John.

How Was the Gospel According to John Written?

In all likelihood, the story of the adulterous woman was added well after the Gospel of John was composed. The evangelists did not work alone. They compiled oral and written testimonies that were handed down by the communities to which they belonged. The Gospel according to John gives particular signs that several authors collaborated in drafting it. For example, we find two very similar conclusions (20:30-31 and 21:24-25), and the narrator sometimes uses the pronoun "we." Scripture scholars suppose that a disciple of Jesus, the one called "the beloved disciple," is the source of this gospel. Over time, tradition has given the name of "John" to this disciple. The Gospel according to John was therefore composed mostly by a second-generation Christian who did not know Jesus. Other contributors also gave a helping hand, including a final editor who would have made changes to arrive at the text we have today. These various collaborators were all part of the same community that created the literary and spiritual masterpiece that is the Gospel according to John.

So the gospels did not fall from the sky. They are the fruit of hard-working writers who wanted to convey their faith. The Church recognized that their texts were both inspired by God and inspiring.

The Adulterous Woman: A Biblical Account?

Although the most reliable manuscripts do not include this narrative, the story of the adulterous woman is considered canonical and inspired. It is certainly one of the latest additions to the Gospel of John. Although the story may have been added later, Christians see a real reflection of the image of Jesus in it. This narrative eventually became part of the New Testament canon thanks to Saint Jerome. Jerome included it in his translation of the Bible, called the Vulgate, a translation that the Catholic Church considered normative. So much the better! For me and many other readers of the New Testament, this is one of the most beautiful pages of the Bible. It shows us that Jesus was willing to challenge the Law, at the risk of his own life, to save a defenseless woman.

An Image of Compassion

The story of the adulterous woman can lead us to reflect on the way we see criminals. Jesus intervened to save a woman who, according to the Law of Moses, deserved death. Jesus breaks the law of his culture, even if that law was perceived as coming from God, to save a person who legally should have been executed.

Not long ago, I attended a lecture by Father Jean Patry, who chose this passage to demonstrate God's love and forgiveness. Father Patry's compassion for prisoners is a powerful witness. He has devoted his life to accompanying those behind bars, whom we prefer to forget. His mission is one of forgiveness, love and reconciliation with rapists, prostitutes and murderers. It is easy to punish people for crimes they have committed. But even the worst criminal remains a human being – and for Father John, they must always be considered children of God. Throughout his life, Father Patry adopted the attitude of Jesus as presented in the story of the adulterous woman. It is encouraging that today, many good people carry out concrete gestures of forgiveness and humanity, like Jesus did.

Entering Jerusalem Seated on Two Donkeys

The Gospel according to Matthew offers us a hilarious scene. Entering Jerusalem, Jesus finds himself sitting at the same time on a donkey and on its colt! Here is the account:

¹When they had come near Jerusalem and had reached Bethphage, at the Mount of Olives, Jesus sent two disciples, ²saying to them, "Go into the village ahead of you, and immediately you will find a donkey tied, and a colt with her; untie them and bring them to me. ³If anyone says anything to you, just say this, 'The Lord needs them.' And he will send them immediately." ⁴This took place to fulfill what had been spoken through the prophet, saying,

> ⁵"Tell the daughter of Zion,
> Look, your king is coming to you,
> humble, and mounted on a donkey,
> and on a colt, the foal of a donkey."

⁶The disciples went and did as Jesus had directed them; ⁷they brought the donkey and the colt, and put their cloaks on them, and he sat on them. ⁸A very large crowd spread their cloaks on the road, and others cut branches from the trees and spread them on the road. ⁹The crowds that went ahead of him and that followed

were shouting, "Hosanna to the Son of David! Blessed is the one who comes in the name of the Lord! Hosanna in the highest heaven!" (Matthew 21:1-9)

Why Two Donkeys?

While the other gospels place Jesus on one donkey, Matthew describes him as being seated on two. This came to be because of Matthew's interpretation of a passage from the book of the prophet Zechariah: "Rejoice greatly, O daughter Zion! Shout aloud, O daughter Jerusalem! Lo, your king comes to you; triumphant and victorious is he, humble and riding on a donkey, on a colt, the foal of a donkey." (Zechariah 9:9) Those who spend time with the psalms know that Hebrew poetry plays a lot on repetition. Here, the word "donkey" is repeated, but it does not necessarily evoke two different animals. The other three gospels reveal an understanding based on a single donkey, which makes much more sense. Yet Matthew sees in Zechariah 9:9 two distinct animals. For him, it is important to show that the prophecy as he understood it was realized. He wasn't concerned about the unlikelihood of the scene.

The essence for Matthew, as for the other gospels, is to demonstrate that the scene as prophesied by Zechariah is an important event. It reveals that Jesus is a humble messiah, unlike the kings and emperors of his time who entered the city on horseback in an extravagant military parade. Jesus simply enters on a donkey (or two). His kingship is different. In the end, the number of donkeys is secondary. What is important is to understand the message conveyed by this somewhat awkward reference to the prophecy of Zechariah.

Looking Back at Life in Light of the Scriptures

In this narrative, Matthew uses a quote from a prophet to show how certain events in the life of Jesus are a fulfillment of the Scriptures. This way of understanding an Old Testament text is not self-evident. The first Christians could understand Jesus better by rereading the Scriptures. By doing so, they were able to see links between the life of Jesus and certain prophetic passages.

Today we can experience a similar situation through the practice of spiritual discernment. Many Christians like to reread the key moments of their lives to discern the presence of God. As readers of the Bible, we can do like the evangelists and reread events through the Scriptures. By opening a common space for the interpretation of our life and the Bible, we move away from an exegetical relationship to the text and gain access to a more personal and spiritual reading. In popular terms, we could compare the Bible to a coach who indicates the direction to follow and the preferred values. One way of doing this personal and spiritual rereading of the Bible is called *lectio divina*. It allows us to see how the Bible is the living word in our lives. In this process we embrace the Bible as the word of God. In the spiritual sphere of life, biblical stories are a kind of alphabet that can enable believers to put their spiritual experiences into words. Our meeting with biblical characters becomes an opportunity to find models on which to build our own identity. The rereading of our life in light of the Bible thus makes it possible to say who we are.

I Am the Donkey

Here is a concrete example: this account of the entrance of Jesus to Jerusalem was very important for one of my friends. In her meditation on this text, like Saint Ignatius suggested, she tried to visualize the scene. Then she threw herself into the heart of it. She identified with the donkey that was tied up until the Lord needed it. This detail in the text allowed her to do a spiritual rereading of her life. She understood that there were times when the Lord had released her from what was restraining her. She allowed herself to be questioned by the narrative to find inner freedom. Like the donkey freed for a specific mission, she now wants to fulfill the mission that she feels God is asking her to do.

Have you ever tried to meditate on a biblical text, to establish a more personal and spiritual relationship with it? Perhaps this type of approach could make you rediscover the Bible in a new way.

Who Carried the Cross?

When reading the gospels, we naturally try to reconcile the four versions of Jesus' life. Yet the attentive reader of the New Testament will notice that many details of the gospels do not agree. For example, who carried the cross of Jesus?

[16]Then the soldiers led him into the courtyard of the palace (that is, the governor's headquarters); and they called together the whole cohort. [17]And they clothed him in a purple cloak; and after twisting some thorns into a crown, they put it on him. [18]And they began saluting him, "Hail, King of the Jews!" [19]They struck his head with a reed, spat upon him, and knelt down in homage to him. [20]After mocking him, they stripped him of the purple cloak and put his own clothes on him. Then they led him out to crucify him.

[21]They compelled a passer-by, who was coming in from the country, to carry his cross; it was Simon of Cyrene, the father of Alexander and Rufus. [22]Then they brought Jesus to the place called Golgotha (which means the place of a skull). [23]And they offered him wine mixed with myrrh; but he did not take it. [24]And they crucified him, and divided his clothes among them, casting lots to decide what each should take. (Mark 15:16-24)

This passage from the Gospel of Mark is clear. It was not Jesus who carried his cross, but Simon of Cyrene, a passerby who had nothing to do with Jesus. Luke and Matthew have another take on this familiar story. Matthew tells us that Simon was walking behind Jesus, suggesting that he was playing the role of a disciple. In fact, Simon of Cyrene is the perfect example of the disciple who hears the call of Jesus and takes up his cross to follow him (Matthew 16:24-28). Let us now look at what the Gospel of John says about the carrying of the cross.

> [14]Now it was the day of Preparation for the Passover; and it was about noon. He said to the Jews, "Here is your King!" [15]They cried out, "Away with him! Away with him! Crucify him!" Pilate asked them, "Shall I crucify your King?" The chief priests answered, "We have no king but the emperor." [16]Then he handed him over to them to be crucified.
>
> So they took Jesus; [17]and carrying the cross by himself, he went out to what is called The Place of the Skull, which in Hebrew is called Golgotha. (John 19:14-17)

The Gospel of John makes no reference to Simon of Cyrene. There are at least two reasons that might explain this. On the one hand, this gospel is the only one that does not insist that the disciples take up their cross and follow Jesus. The character of Simon of Cyrene is therefore not necessary. On the other hand, John presents Jesus in a different way from the three other gospels. For him, Jesus is the Word (*logos*) who became flesh, the messenger of God. The crucifixion in John is not presented as a mere execution, but rather as a means of elevating Jesus to heaven. The Passion according to John shows a Jesus who seems to be so in control of the situation that he carries his own cross.

Who Carried the Cross?

So whom should we believe? Under the pretext that they were written twenty years before the Gospel of John, should we trust the Gospels of Mark, Matthew and Luke, who claim that Jesus did not carry his cross alone? Yet the version of John seems more in line with the way the Romans enacted a crucifixion. Normally, the torturer carried the lateral part of the cross. Finally, a third possible answer can be put forward: Jesus might have carried his cross for part of the way, before being helped by Simon of Cyrene. This is an interesting compromise, but it has the disadvantage of not being based on biblical evidence.

Ultimately, to reconcile the two traditions at any cost is probably not the best solution. Each of these traditions has something to tell us. The first three gospels illustrate the importance of bearing your cross to become a disciple, following Jesus along the path of his Passion. John's account shows that Jesus remains master of the situation, even during his crucifixion. Symbolically, for this gospel, the cross is not only the way Jesus died, but is also the place where he was elevated to the Father. Crucifixion is not the end of history, but rather an important step toward Christ's victory over death.

Praying the Way of the Cross

As a teenager, I sang with the choir of St. Joseph's Oratory in Montreal. The liturgy surrounding the Way of the Cross on Good Friday fascinated me: I could see that the participants associated their own suffering with that of Jesus. Far from being sanitized, this celebration allowed participants to pray with real emotions. I remarked, however, that the fourteen stations of the Way of the Cross did not correspond to what was described in the gospel of the Passion as read on Passion (Palm) Sunday. Among the elements that raise questions are the three falls of Jesus (third, seventh and ninth stations), his meeting with Mary, his mother (fourth station), and Veronica wiping the face of Jesus (sixth station).

Simon of Cyrene makes his appearance at the fifth station. Jesus begins by carrying the cross, and then Simon helps him for part of the way. The Way of the Cross is therefore a perfect illustration of an attempt to reconcile the various narratives of the gospels, in spite of their differences. The stations of the Way of the Cross are rooted in the piety of the end of the medieval period. At that time, people wanted to visualize the details of Jesus' suffering so they could enter into a personal and emotional relationship with the Passion of Christ. The Way of the Cross proved to be very effective. It still achieves this goal by motivating the prayer of millions of Catholics every Friday during Lent.

The Crucifixion: Abandonment and Revelation

The Gospel according to Mark presents a Jesus who dies in complete surrender (15:25-39). This narrative is very different from the other gospels, where Jesus seems to be in control of the situation, forgiving the sin of those who crucify him or conversing with others being crucified with him. In Mark, Jesus remains silent after his condemnation by Pilate. His disciples have all forsaken him. On the cross, the only words attributed to Jesus are in Aramaic, his mother tongue: "At three o'clock Jesus cried out with a loud voice, 'Eloi, Eloi, lema sabachthani?' which means, "My God, my God, why have you forsaken me?" (Mark 15:34). It is far from the crucifixion presented as an accomplishment or as a step toward heaven!

On the cross, Jesus seeks to understand why God has abandoned him, citing the beginning of Psalm 22. This psalm begins with a cry of despair at the anguish of death, but ends with a surprising discovery. The presence of God is near to the one who is crying out. This prayer moves from the feeling of abandonment to the conviction that God is present.

God's Reaction

Was Jesus really abandoned by God? The testimony of the gospels does not end with the crucifixion. God does not leave

Jesus in abandonment. Yet a certain "interventionist" image of God dies with Jesus on the cross. God did not intervene to save him from death.

God's reaction to the execution of Jesus is revealed in the following event: the veil of the Temple is torn apart. According to popular belief, the Temple was the place where God resides on earth. There is a link between this event and the mourning rituals of the time, where a person would tear their own clothing. In a way, we have here the image of a God who enters into mourning, tearing the veil of the Holy of Holies.

A Disconcerting Witness

In Mark, the narrative of the Passion ends with an unexpected phrase: a Roman centurion proclaims that Jesus is the Son of God. Yet the centurion is a pagan and represents the very forces that crucified Jesus. Earlier in the gospel, the title "Son of God" has already been proclaimed by a demon. Now it is a pagan's turn to reveal the identity of Jesus. From the centurion's point of view, crucifixion was not abandonment by God, but rather the revelation of Jesus' divine nature.

God, Suffering and Evil

Many people wonder about the connection between God and human suffering. If God is infinitely good and omnipotent, why does he not intervene to prevent unjust suffering? Does unjust suffering prove that God is not omnipotent, since he does not intervene? Or does unjust suffering prove that God is not good, because he does not intervene? Various explanations have been put forward over the centuries to answer this difficult question.

I dislike this philosophical debate. For me, God's best answer to the question of suffering is the cross. In Jesus, God became incarnate; he became human. There is much talk about the birth of Jesus with reflections on the Incarnation, but his death is just as important. In Jesus, God went through the same suffering and death as we humans do. Suffering and death are part of the human condition. When we must experience these realities, we may ask ourselves, "Where is God?" Reading the stories of the Passion reveals to us that God suffers and dies like us and with us.

Zombies Walking Through Jerusalem

The four gospels give differing accounts of the Passion of Jesus. Most of the main elements overlap, but some interesting details make each story unique. I suggest that you read the crucifixion according to Matthew. This narrative is in line with people's current interests in zombies.

45From noon on, darkness came over the whole land until three in the afternoon. 46And about three o'clock Jesus cried with a loud voice, "Eli, Eli, lema sabachthani?" that is, "My God, my God, why have you forsaken me?" 47When some of the bystanders heard it, they said, "This man is calling for Elijah." 48At once one of them ran and got a sponge, filled it with sour wine, put it on a stick, and gave it to him to drink. 49But the others said, "Wait, let us see whether Elijah will come to save him." 50Then Jesus cried again with a loud voice and breathed his last. 51At that moment the curtain of the temple was torn in two, from top to bottom. The earth shook, and the rocks were split. 52The tombs also were opened, and many bodies of the saints who had fallen asleep were raised. 53After his resurrection they came out of the tombs and entered the holy city and appeared to many. 54Now when the centurion and those with him, who were keeping watch over Jesus, saw the earthquake and what took place, they were terrified and said, "Truly this man was God's Son!" (Matthew 27:45-54)

The Dead Resurrected

The death of Jesus engenders all sorts of apocalyptic phenomena: the veil of the Temple is torn, and an earthquake splits rocks and opens tombs! Dead people rise and walk around Jerusalem. In many ways, this scene unfolds like a horror film. How did the people of Jerusalem react to zombies in their midst? The text does not say, but the reaction of readers today might range from fear to laughter, since this narrative crosses the limits of reality. The laws of nature appear to be temporarily suspended, allowing living beings to rise from the dead. Note that this is a story. And when we read a story, we agree to suspend our disbelief and enter the world of the narrative. This is how we get caught up in movies even if the plot does not pass a reality check. In short, when reading Matthew chapter 27, we must accept this manifestation of "zombies" and consider it as a way of showing the importance of what has just happened: Jesus, the Messiah, has died.

The text says nothing about the nature of the phenomenon. Is it simply resuscitation, like that of Lazarus? Will these people have to die again? Was it the final resurrection? Instead of being with God, the risen dead are walking through Jerusalem, a place associated with death from the beginning of the Gospel of Matthew.

A Biblical Background

The opening of tombs can be related to the parable of the dried bones in Ezekiel 37:12-13:

> ¹²I am going to open your graves, and bring you up from your graves, O my people; and I will bring you back to the land of Israel. And you shall know that I am the Lord, when I open your graves, and bring you up from your graves, O my people.

Following the exile to Babylon, texts like this one used the opening of tombs as a symbol of the return of the Hebrew people to Israel. Similarly, the earthquake can direct us to the text of Zechariah 14:4-5, in which the arrival of the saints from heaven causes an earthquake and collapses the Mount of Olives, announcing God's final judgment. These two Old Testament texts provide a useful background to enable us to better understand the story of Matthew.

Apocalyptic Signs: Signs of Life

The apocalyptic signs in this narrative are both an anticipation of the end of time and the resurrection of the dead. Christians are convinced that the crucifixion is not a catastrophe, but a victory. All the upheavals described in the text bear witness to the greatness of the event – to the death and resurrection of Jesus. Paradoxically, the death of Jesus is a source of life. It makes the resurrection possible. This narrative is a prelude leading us toward the morning of Passover, which is told in the following chapter of the gospel. It should not cause us to react in horror, since it is a sign of hope. What is more, the centurion and the soldiers who attend the scene are fearful and express the conviction that Jesus is the Son of God.

Zombie Jesus Day?

Talking about resurrection in modern times is a challenge. A good friend of mine who did not receive a Christian education keeps telling me jokingly that Jesus is a kind of zombie. If Jesus was crucified and raised up to walk among the living, it is because he came back from the dead by becoming a zombie. Do you think my friend is delirious? Well, there is actually a movement in the United States demanding that Easter be renamed Zombie Jesus Day!

When Christians talk about the resurrection, they cannot act as if everyone understands and believes. To turn the resurrected Christ into a zombie is completely heretical, but this heresy has been caused by the way we speak about the resurrection: we do not take into account the questions our contemporary culture raises on this subject.

Resurrection Questioned

Many elements of the resurrection make it difficult to discuss. First, there is the supernatural element. The resurrection of Jesus is not a historical event that can be proved. Believing is an act of faith. The first Christians tried to convey to us what they understood from their experience. By telling us that Jesus has risen from the dead, they are saying that he who was crucified is no longer in his tomb: he is alive! This is within the realm of believing, not of science. There is an irrational aspect to it. Today we are strongly marked by a rational and scientific mind that prevents us from accepting amazing stories as if they were empirical facts. Christians have the right to believe that this is a real event, but they must be aware that for those who do not have faith, the resurrection is a mere legend.

Our relationship with other religions must also be taken into account. Christians do not have the only discourse on death and the afterlife. Each religion has its own interpretation, and the teachings of Christians, Muslims, Buddhists and others cannot all be true at the same time. For a lot of people, resurrection is only one religious myth among many.

We Are Thomas

Like Thomas, we would like to see and even touch the Risen One to believe in him (John 20:24-28). Unfortunately, it's not possible. Our relationship to the risen Christ is not so direct. But through faith we can see him in the midst of a community that is gathering in his name. We can touch him whenever we continue his mission of inclusion. We can hear him in the silence of prayer.

There is a lot of mystery surrounding the question of resurrection. I share in Christian hope and believe that the elements of doubt present in our culture encourage us to find new and more appropriate ways of speaking about the resurrection. But for goodness' sake, Jesus is neither a ghost nor a zombie! We must make an effort to present him in light of who he is.

Women Deacons, and Bishops with Children

The Greek word *episcopos* means "the one who is watching." At the end of the first century, the episcopate was not yet a structured ministry, but the tasks of the leaders of Christian communities were clearly defined.

Episcopes are the ancestors of the bishops who, even today, are responsible for dioceses. A passage from the first letter to Timothy enumerates the qualities required for a good *episcope*.

[10]And let them first be tested; then, if they prove themselves blameless, let them serve as deacons. [11]Women likewise must be serious, not slanderers, but temperate, faithful in all things. [12]Let deacons be married only once, and let them manage their children and their households well; [13]for those who serve well as deacons gain a good standing for themselves and great boldness in the faith that is in Christ Jesus.

[14]I hope to come to you soon, but I am writing these instructions to you so that, [15]if I am delayed, you may know how one ought to behave in the household of God, which is the church of the living God, the pillar and bulwark of the truth. [16]Without any doubt, the mystery of our religion is great: He was revealed in flesh, vindicated in spirit, seen by angels, proclaimed among

Gentiles, believed in throughout the world, taken up in glory. (1 Timothy 3:10-16)

One element of this passage may surprise contemporary readers. Not only does the first letter to Timothy reveal that *episcopes* could be married, it specifies that they should have only one wife. Rules of conduct are usually set out to redefine a practice. It is highly possible that there were polygamous *episcopes*, and that this practice was not seen in a positive light. The way the *episcope* governed his family was important; it was perceived as a reflection of the way he dealt with the Church. More generally, celibacy was not a common practice among the first ecclesial leaders. The gospels tell us that Jesus healed Peter's mother-in-law: the one who is considered *a posteriori* the first pope had a wife. The importance of celibacy for the ministers of the Church began around the fourth century, but it was not until the thirteenth century that ecclesiastical celibacy became a strict rule.

The first letter to Timothy continues with similar recommendations for deacons:

> [8]Deacons likewise must be serious, not double-tongued, not indulging in much wine, not greedy for money; [9]they must hold fast to the mystery of the faith with a clear conscience. [10]And let them first be tested; then, if they prove themselves blameless, let them serve as deacons. [11]Women likewise must be serious, not slanderers, but temperate, faithful in all things. [12]Let deacons be married only once, and let them manage their children and their households well; [13]for those who serve

well as deacons gain a good standing for themselves and great boldness in the faith that is in Christ Jesus. (1 Timothy 3:8-13)

The records dealing with deacons seem a little less constraining. For example, there is no mention of any regulations in relation to their teaching, probably because their responsibilities were less important than those of the *episcopes*. And yet, the recommendation to have only one wife also applies to them. There is, however, one great difference. Verse 11 introduces particular remarks concerning women. Are these the wives of deacons, or women who were themselves deacons? Both interpretations can be justified. Other biblical texts do mention female deacons. The most famous one is Phoebe, a collaborator of Paul's:

> [1]I commend to you our sister Phoebe, a deacon of the church at Cenchreae, [2]so that you may welcome her in the Lord as is fitting for the saints, and help her in whatever she may require from you, for she has been a benefactor of many and of myself as well. (Romans 16:1-2)

When you look at the first letter to Timothy, one element might strike you by its absence: the letter makes recommendations to the men and women of the congregation, to *episcopes* and deacons, but makes no mention of priests, formerly called presbyters (elders). With time, the ministries of the Church took on the forms we know today. We must not make the mistake of projecting the present structure of ministries in the Church onto the first century of Christianity.

Responsibilities in the Church

A good understanding of the history of the Church allows us to consider how the concept of its ministries evolved. Responsibilities, titles and criteria have changed over time. Which ecclesial ministries does the Church need today? Everyone can see that there is a vocations crisis in the West. What can we do? There are no simple solutions, but I think a working knowledge of the Bible and of the history of ministries can help us in our quest for renewal. The current model of ministries in the Catholic Church has not always been what it is today, and it will continue to evolve. Also, ecumenical dialogue could allow the Catholic Church to be inspired by churches with very different ministerial structures.

Should Women Be Silent?

Paul is often accused of being a misogynist. Indeed, certain passages in his letters do nothing to promote gender equality. Here is one of those excerpts, found among Paul's instructions on proper behaviour in an assembly.

> [34]Women should be silent in the churches. For they are not permitted to speak, but should be subordinate, as the law also says. [35]If there is anything they desire to know, let them ask their husbands at home. For it is shameful for a woman to speak in church. (1 Corinthians 14:34-35)

Was Paul a Misogynist?

For most of us, these verses are profoundly disturbing, to say the least. It is very difficult to reconcile this passage with the notion of equality between men and women, a key principle of our modern society. It would be easy to discredit this passage if Paul had not written it. Yet scripture scholars do not question that Paul penned the first letter to the Corinthians. At best, to save Paul from being labelled a misogynist, we must recall the social context of his time. The culture in which he lived and wrote was a misogynistic one. For a woman to speak out in public at that time was considered out of place.

The Voice of Women in the Assembly

Readers would be justified in raising criticisms about this passage. But can we be sure that all churches followed the practice of forbidding women from speaking out? If women never spoke at the meetings, the question would not have arisen. The fact that Paul denounces the voice of women in an assembly indicates that this practice existed. On the other hand, in this same letter, chapter 11, verse 5, Paul talks about women who pray or prophesy. At this point in the letter, he insists that they must wear a veil on their head when they speak in the assembly. When they speak in the assembly? What a contradiction! (And yes, the wearing of a veil is also part of our Christian tradition. Only sixty years ago, women had to have their heads covered with a scarf or hat to pray in church.)

Interpreting the Bible to Keep Women Silent

To support his ban, Paul evokes the law. But it is difficult to understand which Law or which part of the Torah he is referring to, since silencing women in an assembly is never mentioned in the Old Testament – or at least is never mentioned explicitly. Still, the first letter to Timothy refers to a biblical source to justify the silencing of women:

> [9]also that the women should dress themselves modestly and decently in suitable clothing, not with their hair braided, or with gold, pearls, or expensive clothes, [10]but with good works, as is proper for women who profess reverence for God. [11]Let a woman learn in silence with full submission. [12]I permit no woman to teach

128

or to have authority over a man; she is to keep silent.
(1 Timothy 2:9-12)

I do not know if this interpretation of chapter 3 of the book of Genesis pleases you, but I find it makes Paul say things that go beyond his intentions. And this excerpt from 1 Timothy is even more problematic when it implies that the salvation of women depends on their being mothers and their perseverance in the virtues of faith, love, holiness and modesty. From a contemporary perspective, we can legitimately find this passage demeaning toward women. It does help us to understand the passage in the Law (Torah) that Paul is referring to when he forbids women to speak, but it does not diminish his sexist image.

The last part of the passage from the first letter to the Corinthians quoted above gives women the right to ask their husbands questions, providing that they do this in private, at home. It is the man who must instruct his wife. This vision once again reveals the patriarchal presuppositions of the culture in which this letter was written. The women could not instruct others in the assembly, but they had the right to ask questions of their husbands. This permission is indeed sexist, but at least it gives women some say, even if it is limited. We must hope they asked as many questions as possible to question the entire male-dominated system.

Women and Ministries

Is there a link between Paul's struggle to silence women in the assembly and the fact that the Catholic Church does not allow women to be ordained even today? Much has happened in two thousand years, and yet things do not seem to change.

There is a paradoxical relationship between the Church and women. On the one hand, women tend to be the majority when it comes to church volunteering, teaching children and adults about the faith, and pastoral care. Also, the majority of pastoral mandates by bishops are given to women. Today, they are involved in all fields of pastoral ministry and even hold positions working with the bishops. The Catholic Church would not be very active in society – hospitals, chaplaincies, armed forces, prisons, etc. – if it were not for all these women doing the groundwork. Yet in liturgies, officially, they have no right to comment on the Scriptures. Our present Catholic culture is perhaps closer to that of Paul's time than we would like to admit…

Other churches have made different choices. For example, on December 17, 2014, the first woman was ordained a bishop in the Church of England, where women represent about one third of the clergy. One day I was walking down the street with a group of teenagers on a mission to meet and help people living on the street. We stopped in front of an Anglican church, where a group of homeless people had gathered. During our discussion with them, they told us that they had been sleeping under the portico of the church. Proud to show us their "home," they invited us to enter. As we went in, my students first noticed a rainbow-coloured Pride flag, put there to show the acceptance of all, regardless of their sexual orientation. Then we looked toward a side chapel, where a woman priest was presiding at the liturgy. My Catholic students could not believe their eyes. One of them exclaimed, "What kind of church is this? Welcoming the homeless and gays, and ordaining women as priests?" The experience of visiting an inclusive church contrasted sharply with their image of the Catholic Church.

Slaves, Obey Your Masters!

Today, it goes without saying that slavery is an inhuman practice. At the time of the first Christians, however, slavery was part of the social organization. The socio-economic model of the Roman Empire was based on the use of slaves. That is why some New Testament texts not only treat slavery as a fact of life, but also recommend that slaves be good slaves!

> [5]Slaves, obey your earthly masters with fear and trembling, in singleness of heart, as you obey Christ; [6]not only while being watched, and in order to please them, but as slaves of Christ, doing the will of God from the heart. [7]Render service with enthusiasm, as to the Lord and not to men and women, [8]knowing that whatever good we do, we will receive the same again from the Lord, whether we are slaves or free.
>
> [9]And, masters, do the same to them. Stop threatening them, for you know that both of you have the same Master in heaven, and with him there is no partiality. (Ephesians 6:5-9)

Obedience to Christ

At first glance, this letter, which is attributed to Paul, tells slaves to obey their master. It even encourages them to serve their master as if he were Christ himself! Other letters from Paul evoke this same image. For him, all Christians are called to be servants: servants of Christ.

Subverting Social Divisions

A closer look at the excerpt reveals that this text must have upset the prevailing ideas of the time. Verse 8 says that free people and slaves have the same dignity. Verse 9 even warns masters not to use threats, for God makes no difference among humans, whether they are free or slaves. This statement is nothing less than revolutionary. At that time, slaves belonged to their master and were perceived as sub-humans who would not know what to do with freedom even if they had it. They needed masters to direct them. Society was hierarchical. There were many levels between the emperor and the slaves. Everyone had their place. The authorities, at the top of this pyramid, did everything in their power to ensure that there was no possibility of social protest.

This text reflects a society divided between free human beings and slaves. But for God, this distinction does not exist. From the first centuries of our era, Christianity had great success among the lower social classes because it offered them a dignity equal to that of other members of society. From our twenty-first-century eyes, this text seems to justify slavery, but in fact, it challenges a fundamental principle of the system, claiming that before God, all people are equal. As Paul says in the Letter to the Galatians: "As many of you as were baptized into Christ have clothed yourselves with Christ. There is no longer Jew or

Greek, there is no longer slave or free, there is no longer male and female; for all of you are one in Christ Jesus." (3:27-28)

Reflecting on Slavery with Pope Francis

The first of January is not only the day after New Year's Eve, it is also the World Day of Peace. Peace is more than just the absence of war. On January 1, 2015, Pope Francis launched an invitation to fight against the various forms of slavery, in his message "No longer slaves but brothers and sisters."

There have been times in the history of humankind when slavery was generally accepted and regulated by law. Is slavery merely a scourge from the past? No. If the Pope has taken the trouble to denounce this phenomenon, it is because it still exists. What are the faces of slavery today? They are very diverse, but we can think of workers, even children, who are enslaved in various economic sectors such as domestic work, manufacturing, agricultural labour, mining, and so on. Human trafficking is another terrible form of slavery.

As well, many immigrants are fleeing difficult and dangerous situations. During their journey, they face multiple perils. They are often deprived of their liberty, their possessions are taken from them, and they may even be abused. When they arrive at their destination, they are often held in inhumane conditions. They then agree to live and work under these conditions because they are undocumented and cannot work legally.

Other people, especially minors, are often forced into prostitution and sexual slavery. Some women are sold into forced marriages.

Finally, child soldiers and prisoners of terrorist groups come to mind. All these people and many others are today's slaves.

There is also a lesser-known aspect of slavery, to which we all contribute, often without realizing it. Many of the goods and services we purchase come from companies that use slaves. For example, some cacao beans, which are used to make chocolate, come from countries in West Africa such as Cameroon, Ivory Coast, Ghana, Guinea and Nigeria, which harvest the beans using children who live in inhumane conditions. When we buy chocolate that is not fair trade, we contribute directly to their slavery. Our pension funds are another example. They often take advantage of child labour in Central American mines. The world's mining companies are headquartered in the United States and Canada. The profits they make, through the exploitation of resources, return to the pockets of their shareholders: that is, to us. Many reports also indicate that this exploitation overlooks environmental concerns and the rights of the people who work there.

The call of Pope Francis is significant, both for believers and for non-believers. Indeed, he uses the metaphor of siblings to remind us of the bonds that unite all human beings. For him, we are all brothers and sisters. Thus, we must respect the dignity, autonomy and freedom of others to fight the exploitation of human beings.

What can we do to fight against slavery? States must continue to ensure that their legislation against exploiting people is implemented. Companies must ensure that their employees have decent working conditions and adequate wages. But ultimately, the responsibility is ours. We as consumers can exercise real power through our purchases. Do you know where and under what conditions the clothes you buy are made? Do you know where to get fair-trade products like coffee, chocolate and bananas? Are you aware of the contents of your pension funds?

At New Year's, rather than making resolutions about losing weight, I urge you to commit to making a difference by changing what you eat, buy or wear. By purchasing products that have not been manufactured by exploiting vulnerable people, we can build a world based on family bonds and solidarity. Let us work together to prolong the World Day of Peace throughout the entire year.

A Pregnant Woman Fights a Dragon

The book of Revelation, also known as the Apocalypse, is written in a literary genre that seems foreign to us. Understanding this text is difficult because of the many images, symbols and allusions to Old Testament texts. Yet these are the elements that make this mysterious book appealing, even for non-believers.

> [1]A great portent appeared in heaven: a woman clothed with the sun, with the moon under her feet, and on her head a crown of twelve stars. [2]She was pregnant and was crying out in birth pangs, in the agony of giving birth. [3]Then another portent appeared in heaven: a great red dragon, with seven heads and ten horns, and seven diadems on his heads. [4]His tail swept down a third of the stars of heaven and threw them to the earth. Then the dragon stood before the woman who was about to bear a child, so that he might devour her child as soon as it was born. [5]And she gave birth to a son, a male child, who is to rule all the nations with a rod of iron. But her child was snatched away and taken to God and to his throne; [6]and the woman fled into the wilderness, where she has a place prepared by God, so that there she can be nourished for one thousand two hundred sixty days.

[7]And war broke out in heaven; Michael and his angels fought against the dragon. The dragon and his angels fought back, [8]but they were defeated, and there was no longer any place for them in heaven. [9]The great dragon was thrown down, that ancient serpent, who is called the Devil and Satan, the deceiver of the whole world—he was thrown down to the earth, and his angels were thrown down with him...

[13]So when the dragon saw that he had been thrown down to the earth, he pursued the woman who had given birth to the male child. [14]But the woman was given the two wings of the great eagle, so that she could fly from the serpent into the wilderness, to her place where she is nourished for a time, and times, and half a time. [15]Then from his mouth the serpent poured water like a river after the woman, to sweep her away with the flood. [16]But the earth came to the help of the woman; it opened its mouth and swallowed the river that the dragon had poured from his mouth. [17]Then the dragon was angry with the woman, and went off to make war on the rest of her children, those who keep the commandments of God and hold the testimony of Jesus. (Revelation 12:1-9, 13-17)

Who is this mysterious pregnant woman, clothed with the sun, who has the moon under her feet and her head crowned with twelve stars? As a good Catholic, I tend to say, "It's Mary." But is it clearly Mary?

First, without a doubt, this passage can be aligned with Genesis 3, where the narrator promises that the offspring of a woman will be victorious over the serpent. The Bible begins with a narrative that shows how a woman was deceived by a serpent and ends with another passage where a woman throws a dragon to the ground.

It is an interesting possibility to see the woman as representing the people of God – she who gives birth to the messiah and to all believers. Like the people who lived through the Exodus, this woman spends time in the desert and is guided by God's providence. The prophets Isaiah (chapters 54 and 60) and Hosea (2:19-21) used the figure of a woman to represent the people as the bride of the Lord. Here, in the New Testament, it could be that a female figure represents the Church, the people of God.

Since this woman is pregnant with the child who takes on a messianic role, it is also certainly possible to see her as a symbolic representation of Mary.

The other key figure, the dragon, is clearly identified with Satan and therefore represents evil – also called "the ancient serpent," it symbolizes the primordial evil forces.

Mary versus the Woman of the Apocalypse

What is the meaning of this scene? The book of Revelation contains several visions experienced by John, a man in exile on the island of Patmos. Through his account, which overflows with symbolic language, he attempts to put into words realities that are inaccessible to ordinary mortals. Naturally, the result is a text that lends itself to various interpretations. Regardless of the identity of the woman, the important element is the victory of God and the defeat of evil. Therefore, we can read this text as an inspiration in our struggle against the various forms of evil we face.

On an organized trip to Ecuador with my students, we saw one of the most famous images of the woman from Revelation. She is standing on the summit of the highest hill of Quito, the capital city. She is easily recognizable with her crown of twelve stars, standing on a crescent moon, with a dragon in chains under her feet. This forty-one-metre-high woman overlooks the city, a reminder of her important place in the Catholic faith.

The statue of Quito represents the great and almost cosmic role of the woman of Revelation. But does she appropriately represent Mary? It all depends on how we see the mother of Jesus. I confess that my favourite depiction of Mary is the one expressed in the Magnificat (Luke 1:46-56). In this anthem, Mary expresses her joy in the works of the Lord. Far from being a prayer in "the clouds," this cry contains a real concern for social justice: "He [the Lord] has brought down the powerful from their thrones, and lifted up the lowly; he has filled the hungry with good things, and sent the rich away empty." In this passage, Mary is shown as a woman who dares to glorify the righteousness of God, a justice that destabilizes the economic and political powers of her time. Unlike the great statue that dominates the city of Quito, Mary of the Magnificat presents herself as a humble servant who counts on God's intervention when faced with the injustices perpetrated by the powerful.

Claude Lacaille, a missionary priest during the dictatorship in Chile, rediscovered the image of Mary with a group of women. Her face was similar to that of these women, who were working as servants for slave wages. Like Mary, these women lived with the hope that the Lord would dethrone the powerful. Here is what they said to my friend Claude:

We are certain that Mary experienced the same misery as Chilean women. She became pregnant when she was still very young and everyone pointed the finger in accusation. It happens to many young girls here, a difficult way to begin the life of a couple. She had no house to receive her child; she had to give birth in a barn, in the greatest poverty. Like many of our compatriots, she suffered from the repression of Herod and had to take refuge at night in another country. Do you envision her riding on the back of a donkey, dressed like a queen with her golden crown? On her return to her village, do you think she was not afraid when the villagers chased Jesus out of the synagogue and wanted to push him off the cliff? Shame! These people were relatives, neighbours who completely rejected what Jesus had to say. How do you think Mary felt when they arrested Jesus and detained him at the high priest's house? We, the Chilean women, know. We have lived it. They attacked our houses in the middle of the night. Hooded men armed with machine guns burst in, overturned everything, scared the children and took away our sons or husbands. It was impossible to know where they were imprisoned.

Often they disappeared forever and we did not know what became of them. When they murdered her only son, Mary stood at the foot of the cross with many other women in view of the executioners. We, the women of Chile, are accustomed to that. We women have faced horror but we are strong.

No, my father, your image of Mary, you can keep her. We have always known that Mary was a woman of the people subjected to all kinds of violence. She stood strong and believed that God would intervene to make change. She fought to raise a rebellious son like us. We see ourselves in this song of Mary. She resembles us when we shout slogans during demonstrations: "Bread, work, justice and freedom," or "Out with Pinochet!" That is why we are fighting. The generals and the rich get richer, and at home unemployment reigns. We go to bed hungry. The children go to school with an empty belly and it is to the bread line that we must go to seek a little food.[6]

I am not a woman. I do not live in a dictatorship. I am not poor. But I can see clearly that there are unacceptable situations in our world and even in North America. I turn to the prophetic words of Mary to have the courage to denounce what is unacceptable, to build a better world and to fight the evil dragons of our society.

---

6   This quote is a translation of Claude Lacaille's article "En marche ! Vous nêtes pas seules ! ": http://www.interbible.org/interBible/source/justice/2014/bjs_141219.html.

Conclusion

At the end of this journey into the heart of strange tales of the Bible, where do we go from here? I hope that by coming into contact with these texts, you were surprised or maybe even laughed a little. But the goal was not just to amuse you. Each biblical passage was copied by thousands of hands before it reached us. The effort that was made should involve some serious reflection on our part. These texts, although unusual, can help us better understand the Bible, God and witnesses of faith from another time. They give us an opportunity to reflect on ourselves and our present culture. The strangest texts of the Bible require us to take time, stop, reread and seek related passages to understand what is at stake. Thank you for spending your time with me and for embarking on this long and rich journey into the history of religion and humankind as transmitted to us through the Bible.

I hope you're hooked… Who knows, maybe this ancient book that is the Bible will be your next reading adventure. It is up to you to choose a biblical book and read the whole thing, by yourself or with someone you love. You may discover a hidden treasure there. Happy reading!